'Whenever I have talked with J[...]
listened to him minister publicly [...]
of someone who authentically lives the passion for prayer that he encourages in others. In *Life on Fire* that passion permeates every page. You will be challenged and inspired as you walk through the pages that follow.'

John Glass
Author, Leadership Consultant, Speaker
General Superintendent, Elim Pentecostal churches
1999–2016

'*Life On Fire* is a book that will disturb all passivity, challenge all double standards, and stir a fresh desperation for God's power to be unleashed. Read and be ready!'

Rachel Hickson
Heartcry for Change

'*Life on Fire* is a key book for this season that the people of God now find themselves in. James expresses a clear voice that carries a clarion call for these times. Out of an apostolic calling upon him for prayer and intercession, he has written this prophetic manual addressing the condition of the modern church and her role in this critical moment. I found myself being personally stirred and challenged. Insightful, prophetic, and hunger-provoking, this book is a must-read for every believer who has set their heart on consecration to the Lord.

These pages have stirred my heart afresh and fanned the flames within it, and I know they will do the same for every reader who takes time to digest the truth they hold.'

Andy Elmes
Lead Pastor of Family Church, Evangelist and Author

'As one who has battled the principality called Jezebel for decades and written several books on the topic, I can tell you James is offering some valuable insight into this wicked spirit in this book. Whether or not you realize it, you have probably contended with the Jezebel spirit. This book offers fresh insights into who Jezebel is and how to break her attacks on your life.'

Jennifer LeClaire
Author, *The Spiritual Warrior's Guide to Defeating Jezebel*
Founder, Awakening House of Prayer Global Movement

'James starts and stokes fires wherever he goes because he's consistently lived a life on fire – and if you read this book with an open heart, I believe you will also experience the fire of God in your life. Your friends, family and community need you to be ablaze with the power of the Holy Spirit and I believe this book could be the spiritual equivalent of a box of matches to get you started.'

Mark Pugh
Lead Pastor, Rediscover Church, Exeter

'A very honest account of two people's journey in their pursuit of knowing the presence, passion and power of God the Father, God the Son and God the Holy Spirit. *Life on Fire* will encourage everyone who reads it to either start or continue on their journey in pursuit of knowing the glorious presence of the divine Trinity in their day to day lives. There is no greater pursuit.'

Ian Cole
World Prayer Centre

'This book will take you on a journey into a reinvigorated lifestyle of devotion and understanding of Jesus. You will learn from James' personal life experiences and gain insight into rhythms of how to be set apart for God. I heartily recommend this book.'

Emma Stark
Director, Global Prophetic Alliance and Glasgow Prophetic Centre, and Leader, British Isles Council of Prophets
Author of *The Prophetic Warrior*

'I believe James Aladiran is one of the bright beacons that God has raised up to proclaim the message of Christ through the vehicle of prayer in this generation. As you read this volume, may the grace for prayer and a sold out attitude come upon you for revival, renewal and the vision of Jesus for all humanity.'

Jonathan Oloyede
National Day of Prayer

LIFE ON FIRE

Becoming a person of
prayer, purity and power

JAMES ALADIRAN

LIFE ON FIRE
Published by Prayer Storm Publishing
prayerstorm.org

© 2021 James Aladiran

ISBN 978-1-8384543-0-2
eISBN 978-1-8384543-1-9

The Team: Simon Baker, Alistair Metcalfe, Emily Shore
Cover design and typesetting: Simon Baker at Thirteen Creative

Printed in the UK.

This book is dedicated to this generation.
We have had many struggles and have been attacked on
many sides by the enemy but we will not be stopped in our
pursuit of God and his assignment for us here on earth.
We were born for such a time as this.
May his will be done in and through us as we prepare the
way for the greatest outpouring of his Spirit.

CONTENTS

ACKNOWLEDGEMENTS

Thanks to my parents, Eileen and Emmanuel Aladiran, who have been great role models, brought me up in the ways of the Lord, and always supported and prayed for me as I followed the calling of God on my life. I'm grateful to my wife, Rebecca Aladiran, who played a massive role in encouraging me to write this book. There were several times when I wanted to give up but your prophetic voice of encouragement kept me going. Many insights and revelations in this book came during our private conservations together and I'm thankful to the Lord for the spirit of wisdom he has given you.

Pamela Maroa and Chidozie Ewuzie: thank you for all your input and encouragement in the early stages of this project. I sincerely appreciate the countless hours you gave in helping me put together my first draft. Alistair Metcalfe, I'm so thankful that you were a part of this journey; your wisdom and contribution to this book have been truly invaluable. Simon Baker, I am thankful for your creativity and overall expertise in making the process of releasing my first book such a positive experience. Thanks to Emily Shore for your work in editing the manuscript. Anna Tran, you made yourself available to help me with some critical sections of the book and I am truly grateful. Pastor Joe Reeser, I am so thankful for your incredible wisdom and I appreciate you making yourself available to help me with parts of this book. Thank you to my wife's parents, Simon and Jane Sullivan, for being instrumental in helping me embark on this writing journey. Collette Dallas, thank you for being a consistent prophetic voice of encouragement to me and my family over this last decade. You have been used by God in such powerful ways in our lives and I'm thankful to the Lord for you. Pastor Paul Lloyd and John Maroa, thank you for your input and wisdom in key parts of this book. Pastors Paul and Janet Booth, thank you for how you supported my family in prayers throughout this journey.

To the amazing Prayer Storm community – our intercessors, singers, musicians, staff, volunteers, trustees, and partners – thank you so much for being living examples of what this book has to say. It is an honour to seek the Lord with you all and I am thankful that God sent you to run alongside us as we believe for him to move in our nation and across the nations.

FOREWORD

Lou Engle

Twenty-one years ago, I received a dream. At the time, I was in the process of mobilizing for TheCall DC, where 400,000 young people gathered to fast and pray for America. In the dream, I was overwhelmed with the impossibility of America turning back to the Lord. Then, a scroll rolled down before me and I read Luke 1:17, describing the Nazirite calling of John the Baptist: 'He shall go on before the Lord in the spirit and power of Elijah to turn the hearts of the fathers to the children and the rebellious to the wisdom of the righteous.' I awoke to the whisper of the Lord, 'What I'm pouring out in America is stronger than the rebellion.' Over the course of the last 21 years, as I've witnessed fields, arenas, and stadiums filled with saints fasting and calling on God, I have often inquired of him, 'Where is the fulfillment of that word?' It seems the rebellion only gets stronger and stronger. But is not this the turning that the book of Malachi promises? Before the great and dreadful day of the Lord, when the nations are in full rebellion, God declares, 'Behold, I will send you the prophet Elijah!' John the Baptist was the first installment of that coming of Elijah and we may now be entering the final installment in preparation for the return of Christ.

What I have beheld in James Aladiran's life, and have just read in the pages of this book, is one of the greatest encouragements to me that the Elijah revolution is now on. That my prayers, and the prayers of my generation, are being answered. In this book, I hear the sound of the 'something stronger!' I wrote a little book some years ago, called *Nazirite DNA*, in which I said:

> No other message that I have preached has been more endorsed prophetically and supernaturally than the call of the Nazirite. It has been foundational to TheCall and to a prayer movement that has erupted among young people in the last 20 years. I believe that a return to Nazirite type consecration is the only hope for a return to God in America and it will be the ground preparation, even the forerunner, for the greatest spiritual awakening she has ever seen.

Life on Fire takes that message to a whole new level, and way beyond the boundaries of America. I truly rejoice and am deeply honored that in some measure my life and message have helped frame James and his wife Rebecca's lives and message.

But know this: the son has surpassed a father. I don't think I've ever been so convicted and challenged by a book or a spoken message. This book has thrown me into a late-life crisis, a life assessment, if you will. I'm in delete mode. I've written of the Elijah Nazirite generation that, 'A high calling demands a commensurate high consecration. Others can but I cannot, I've been called to higher purposes.' I've tried to live out those higher purposes, but have at times allowed the 'I cans' of other things, even seemingly good things, to dim the fires of my soul. As Jim Elliot, the great missionary martyr to the Auca Indians, said, 'Am I ignitable? God deliver me from the dread asbestos of other things. Let me not sink to be a clod, make me thy fuel oh flame of God!' What keeps me from burning? James' book has provoked me to find the asbestos in the walls of my spiritual house, this earthly temple, and tear it out.

Deletion by grace, not by law! Drawn by superior eternal pleasures and greater eternal rewards, the Elijah prophet pilgrim presses through the gravitational barriers that bind the soul to earth and thereby finds the life on fire, the winged life of fasting, and the exhilarating flight of faith. A life on fire is how Jesus described John the Baptist: 'He was a burning and shining lamp!' (John 5:35). When will this kind of Christianity light up the earth? The Spirit of Holiness in James' life and his burning book is kindling for such a conflagration. 'Those who sat in darkness have seen a great light' (Isaiah 9:2).

Maybe the turning of the hearts of the fathers to the children, and the turning of the hearts of the children to the fathers is something like this. The sons read and hear the stories and the faith of the fathers. Then they respond in a double portion of grace and consecration. Then the fathers, watching and reading of the faith and the stories of the sons, are provoked to return to their original burn and relight their candles to the torch of the new breed. This is surely what has happened to me. I want to be like James when I grow up.

This burning book, packed with biblical and prophetic dream revelation, illuminates with blazing clarity Elijah's narrative and inspires great inward desires to live holy and wholly for God. Oh that a whole generation would read this book and run into this promised coming of Elijah. A pseudo-Christianity in England, America, the West, is spiritually reeling under the invasion of thought systems, lies, and inauthentic lifestyles that are hostile to biblical truth and are luring a young generation into a mass spirit of delusion. In this technological age of instant Instagram pseudo prophets, much of what we hear is just noise, noise, noise! We don't need more noises; what we need are voices. Prophets are forged in the deserts of fasting, not the desserts of feasting. We've called our children to feast and play, but the times demand that they fast and pray. John was in the desert until the day of his public appearance. James, you are a voice calling out in this spiritual wilderness of the West and it is my hope – perhaps a prophecy – that this book, your message, and your movement will bring forth a corporate Man on Fire that will prepare the way for the coming of Christ in the world's greatest global spiritual awakening.

Lou Engle, January 2021

FOREWORD

Karen Wheaton

I t was Winter Ramp 2017. The Ramp auditorium was filled with over 1,000 mostly young men and women who had set themselves to seek God and worship their way into the new year. Although the conference was going well, I could sense some sort of resistance in the spiritual atmosphere that I didn't quite understand. We continued to worship, dance, shout and praise, knowing from experience that the weapon of worship often brings the desired breakthrough. This time, however, after four services, the strange atmosphere remained. Concerned, and leaning in to hear anything that God might be saying, I called James Aladiran to the platform to release the word God had given him for the conference.

As he began to preach this prophetic message, unveiling the hidden spirit of Jezebel and revealing the identity of this Jehu generation, something began to break – or, should I say, shatter – the resistance. Young men and women literally rushed the altars, wailing in repentance, as the influence of this spirit was broken off their lives! I will never forget their faces as tears were flowing from the deepest places of their hearts. Nor will I forget the joy that exploded in their worship from the revelation of their freedom. From that point on, the conference shifted.

For the past 20 plus years, I have worked closely with young people, mostly high school and university students. I have seen first hand how the enemy has eroded their innocence, stolen their identity, and led them down paths of addiction with the intent to utterly destroy their lives. At the click of a button, the most heinous and pornographic excesses are laid bare before the vulnerable eyes of our children until, as they describe it, 'It hooked me, and it hooked me deep.' With their self-worth destroyed and with no hope of ever breaking free of this tormenting, mysterious darkness, many contemplate or turn to suicide as their only option for escape.

Even as Christian leaders and parents, we find ourselves fighting for the very souls of our own sons and daughters, and searching for answers about how to reach them. 3 John 4 says, 'I have no greater joy than to hear that my children walk in truth.' I am sure many parents can attest to this, but we also know that the reverse is equally true: there is no greater sorrow for Christian parents than to see our children bound in deception and rebellion. In pain and confusion, we ask ourselves, 'What has happened to my child?' 'What and who is this unseen enemy that I am at war with?'

I believe the message of this book contains answers to many of our questions and gives us the key to unlock the chains that have held our children in bondage for generations. Luke 11:21 says, 'When a strong man, fully armed, guards his own house, his possessions are safe. But when someone stronger attacks and overpowers him, he takes away the armour in which the man trusted and divides up his plunder.' The 'Stronger One' is about to step off the pages of this book and empower you to rise up with a new boldness in prayer and authority, resulting in deliverance for you and those you love.

James Aladiran has received this word by revelation of the Holy Spirit. He lives and preaches this message as a burning man of God. Let him who has an ear, truly hear what the Spirit is saying! I believe I can hear the sound of galloping...

Karen Wheaton, January 2021

MY 11:11 MOMENT

There are moments in our lives when God gives us a glimpse of who he is and we are forever changed. I have come to realise that these encounters are often used by God to accomplish a lot more in us than we recognise at the time. Only with hindsight do we see more clearly how God has been at work in our lives, even when we had no idea what was going on.

November 11, 2009 is etched in my mind as one of those life-defining moments of encounter with the Lord. It was also extra special for me because it was my birthday. I had woken early in the morning to pray and my iPod (remember those?) was connected to some speakers in my bedroom, but I had no music playing. All of a sudden, while I was praying, a song randomly started to play. At first I was startled by this, wondering at how bizarre it was that the iPod seemed to have a mind of its own, but as the song played I found myself in floods of tears, encountering God in a way I had never done before.

The song that the iPod seemed to have chosen on a whim was one by Eddie James called 'Prepare the Way'. On this particular version of the track, Lou Engle, an intercessor for revival and co-founder of TheCall, is praying as Eddie James sings. I listened as Lou exhorted the teenagers at the Winter Ramp 2006 gathering:

> I want us to pray for something to come forth this year of a spiritual awakening we have never seen before... pray for your generation, that it would be said in the future that a great generation came forth from the south and overthrew the altars of Baal, overthrew the altars of sexual immorality, overthrew the altars of abortion and brought forth the greatest awakening in the history of America.

Then he went on to pray:

> God, we are crying out for a moral resurgence out of the south, turn the nation back to you, let it begin here. God, we pray for the greatest awakening in the history of America; rip the veil, God...

As Lou prays on the track, Eddie James sings these lyrics:

> Prepare, prepare, prepare ye the way of the Lord, for
> the kingdom is at hand and I'm coming with power
> and glory to this land. Prepare ye the way of the Lord.

I was listening to this in Manchester, England, and even though the prayers were very much focused on America, somehow it felt like everything in me was connecting to it profoundly. I could feel deep groans within my heart as the presence of God intensified in my bedroom. I couldn't stop weeping as I knew God was speaking to me.

For several months before this day, it had seemed to me that everywhere I turned I could see this pattern of numbers, 11:11. I just couldn't escape from it. I had even started to get a bit concerned, wondering what was wrong with me, but at the same time I couldn't shake off an inexplicable sense that there was something really significant about these numbers. Many times over the period of about two months, while praying, I would open my eyes and the time would be 11:11am, 1:11pm, or the numbers 11:11 would be in front of me. It all seemed really weird, to be honest! I kept wondering if God was trying to get my attention but I had no idea why 11:11 should be so significant.

But on my birthday, which happened to be 11/11 – November 11 – it all began to make sense. Right there in my bedroom on my 26th birthday, overcome by the presence of God, I was being awakened to a calling I knew little about. With hindsight, it seems to me as though something from heaven was stirred up within me that I have found myself still unravelling and unable to shake off all these years later.

I have often felt drawn to the character of John the Baptist, without fully knowing why. Reading through the gospels of Matthew, Mark, Luke and John I have been inspired by John's intense devotion to the Lord, and how he played such a significant role in preparing the way for Jesus. As I took time to reflect on what the Lord was doing in me on my birthday it occurred to me to look up Matthew 11:11, and to my surprise it was a scripture about John the Baptist:

> Assuredly, I say to you, among those born of women there has not risen one greater than John the Baptist; but he who is least in the kingdom of heaven is greater than he.
>
> — Matthew 11:11

This scripture shed some light on why I had been seeing 11:11 all around me. It seemed to me that the Lord was drawing my attention to the life of John the Baptist. And even though, at the time, I didn't have a lot of understanding of the significance of John's life, I somehow knew that his lifestyle painted a prophetic picture of what God was calling me to.

So, there I was in my bedroom on my birthday, 11/11, and the Lord was speaking to me about Matthew 11:11 – how amazing is that? John the Baptist was a man of fasting and prayer; he was radical in his devotion to the Lord. I had seen the Lord stir my heart for prayer, and at this time in my life

I was accustomed to fasting often. However, after the encounter with the Lord on my birthday, I began to sense that he was calling me to a new level of intensity in fasting. It was a clear call to fast for 40 days on water and liquids. I was really concerned about going on this fast, thinking: 'Lord, I'm already skinny, what will be left of me after 40 days of no food!' As I was going back and forth about this in my head, I received a text from my friend and intercessor Jane Sullivan – who would later become my mother-in-law – asking if I would consider doing a 40-day fast, starting in January 2010. I took this as confirmation that the Lord was truly calling me to do this – I mean, how often do you get a text from someone asking you to join them in a 40-day fast?

Such an extended period of fasting wasn't completely new to me. My first ever 40-day fast was what's often called a Daniel fast – eating vegetables, with no meats or sweets – and I did this in the summer of 2007. It actually changed the trajectory of my life. I believe everything I do now in ministry was birthed in those 40 days. But as much I had some experience of different types of fasts, I had never yet been involved in 40 days of fasting only on water and liquids. So it took me some time to say yes to the Lord on this one.

However, as soon as I resolved in my heart to obey, some unusual confirmations began to fall into place. First, the Lord used Debra Green. Debra leads an organisation here in the UK called 'Redeeming our Communities', which focuses on crime reduction through partnerships with the police, churches, community groups and other organisations. She was praying for me at the time, unaware of what the Lord had been saying to me about John the Baptist. As soon as she started praying, she told me that she felt the Lord saying, 'A voice of one in the wilderness crying, "Prepare the way of the Lord."' She went on to say, 'I feel like this is going to involve fasting.'

In John 1, we find John the Baptist being questioned about his identity by some individuals who were sent by the Pharisees:

> Then they said to him, 'Who are you, that we may give an answer to those who sent us? What do you say about yourself?' He said: 'I am the voice of one crying in the wilderness: "Make straight the way of the Lord," as the prophet Isaiah said.'
>
> — John 1:22–23

The prophetic word from Debra confirmed to me the connection between the fast I was about to embark upon and John the Baptist's calling to prepare the way of the Lord.

A few weeks after this, I was talking to a friend at work (who, again, had no idea what had been happening), and he looked at the flyer for an event called 'Prayer Storm', which I was organising at the time, and pointed out to me that the meeting was going to last for 11 hours. I hadn't even noticed that. I began to describe to him how I had been seeing 11:11 everywhere and he said, 'Wow! I saw that number this morning as I was praying and didn't know what it meant, so I guess it's linked to this somehow!'

Right after this conversation with my friend, I turned on my phone and guess what the time was? 1.11pm. The number really was showing up in the most bizarre places – checking email on my phone later that day, the screen said 'Downloading 11 of 11 messages'! You get the picture...

Through all these unusual and unlikely confirmations, God was leaving me in no doubt that he was calling me to live a 'John the Baptist' lifestyle of prayer and fasting. But I knew it wasn't just about me – it was a call to a generation across the nations of the earth to be forerunners like John the Baptist, to fill up the valleys, bringing the mountains and high places low, making the crooked paths straight and rough ways smooth. The Lord is raising up radical warriors in this generation, who will set themselves apart for him, seek his face with a tunnel vision – with consistency and fervency, without compromise – and they will usher in the greatest awakening the world has ever seen.

In response to these prophetic words and encounters with the Lord, the Prayer Storm team and I called a 40-day fast that began on January 11, 2010 and ended with a 'solemn assembly' Prayer Storm gathering on February 21, 2010. We saw many teenagers and young adults from across our region join us in prayer and fasting for our city of Manchester and for the United Kingdom. We came together, believing for God to raise up forerunners across the land who would be like John in their devotion to Jesus, wholly given to a lifestyle of fasting and prayer – a generation that would overthrow the altars of sexual immorality across the land and usher in the glory of the King.

There is a strong connection between John the Baptist and Elijah. In the book of Luke 1:11-19 we read about an encounter that John's dad, Zechariah, had with the angel Gabriel, when he was told that John would 'go on before the Lord, in the spirit and power of Elijah.' As we will explore later on, Elijah didn't complete his assignment, and John the Baptist was beheaded. Both Elijah and John were up against a wicked spirit that worked through personalities, governmental structures and systems to oppose, frustrate, contaminate and ultimately annihilate the prophetic move of God. From the encounter I had on my birthday, I knew the Lord was drawing my attention to John the Baptist and the ways in which he was used by God in his generation. However, knowing that both Elijah and John had been essentially 'taken out' by the same spirit, I felt there was a lot that I needed to learn from their journeys in order to be effective in God's calling on my life.

This is where you come in.

There are spiritual forces that seek to oppose and frustrate the advancement of the army of God. Therefore, the army the Lord is raising up must be strong and equipped for battle. We need to be aware of the forces of darkness that seek to oppose the coming of the kingdom of God in our generation. We cannot afford to be ignorant of the working of this same spirit that opposed Elijah and also caused John the Baptist to be beheaded. It is a spirit of seduction – it is the spirit of Jezebel.

LIFE ON FIRE

In this book, I intend to bring a fresh perspective on the fore-running generation we're part of and the workings of the spirit of Jezebel in our society at large. I believe that this revelation will bring great hope and deliverance to many individuals who are called to be forerunners like John the Baptist, and who (often times in ignorance) have come under the influence and dominance of this spirit. According to Jesus in Revelation 2:26, those who overcome this spirit are given authority over nations. My desire in writing on this subject is not just to see individuals step into a place of personal freedom, but to see the Church arise to be a true agent of regional and national transformation, walking in authority over nations.

In Part One, through scripture and some personal experiences, we will take a look at some of the manifestations of the spirit of Elijah as it pertains to the life of John the Baptist. We will also begin to shine a light on the workings of the spirit of Jezebel. In Part Two, we will be delving deeper by looking at what Jesus had to say about Jezebel and the working of this spirit in popular culture. In Part Three, through the epic story of Jezebel's destruction in 2 Kings 9, we will explore some strategies for destroying the influence of this spirit in our lives and in society at large.

Over the years, I have heard many interpretations from different people of what '11:11' means. I am not claiming to have the only, definitive interpretation, but I do know beyond a shadow of a doubt that the Lord was using this as a sign to get my attention, pointing to the revelation of what he was and is doing in our generation, and that is what I want to share here.

John the Baptist came in the spirit of Elijah, and one of the manifestations of the spirit of Elijah is a spirit of intercession. Elijah was a man of intensity and tenacity in prayer. Simply put, Elijah had prayer stamina. I believe John was also a man of great stamina in prayer. In Luke 11:1, Jesus' disciples asked him to teach them to pray just as John taught his disciples.

We desperately need an increase in our prayer stamina in the 21st century Church. The workings of the spirit of Elijah in the life of John the Baptist enabled him to go into the throne room of God, receive what was on God's mind, and birth it in the earth through the womb of intercession. John is a prototype of the generation that the Lord is raising up in these last days. The number 11:11 speaks of that generation, which I believe is this generation.

On my birthday, the Lord birthed in me a calling to 'prepare the way', in fasting and prayer, for a move of his Spirit in my generation. That encounter also awakened me to what I believe is one of the most critical battles the people of God will face on the earth in the end times, before the return of Jesus. This book is about what I have learned and how it has changed me.

Perhaps you, like me, desire to be part of the Lord's army to prepare the way for what he wants to do in our generation. As you read this book, I pray the Lord will birth in you the same passion he birthed in me to do just that. I believe you will be empowered to overcome the devices of the enemy that are seeking to oppose the prophetic move of God in the earth today, and that you will be challenged and inspired to live a life on fire.

PART ONE

THE SPIRIT OF ELIJAH

CHAPTER ONE

WAKING UP

Break free from spiritual slumber

Marriage can be a journey of self-discovery (and some discoveries are more painful than others!). I have been married for eight years now, and my wife tells me I have changed a lot in that time, which I take as an encouragement!

One thing I never realised until I got married was just how intense I can be. For example, for our honeymoon we went to Morocco. We had such a wonderful time together. But after the first week I started to feel unsettled and was ready to get back home. Now, I don't remember saying these exact words, but my wife Rebecca reminded me recently that after week one of our honeymoon I told her I was depressed and felt like my life was wasting away. After eight years of marriage I have had a powerful revelation that most married people will eventually have: your spouse will remember the exact wording of everything you'd rather forget you ever said!

Rebecca helped me to realise that I was used to living such an intense life that a two week holiday was a challenge for me, even though it was my honeymoon. Thankfully, I'm a lot different now, but I know I can still be intense in many ways. Often, in the middle of a conversation, when I was clearly reaching extreme levels of intensity, Rebecca would say, 'James, you're being a ten when you need to be a two.'

Has anyone ever referred to you as an 'intense' person? However intense we are, John the Baptist took it to a whole new level. I mean he lived in the desert, wearing camel's hair and a leather belt. He had a strange diet of locusts and wild honey (which is pretty much a fast if you think about it), and then on top of that, he fasted often. So, basically, he broke his strange diet of locusts and wild honey to eat nothing! Now that's intense.

John's father, Zechariah, was a priest so John would have been expected to follow in his father's footsteps, serving the Lord in the temple. There is nothing in the Old Testament scriptures commanding him to eat locusts and wild honey in order to be devoted to God. So why did John choose to live such an intense life?

I believe one of the reasons was that the culture around John had been in such a place of compromise, darkness and lack of prophetic revelation for many years. In order to shift the nation from its compromise, God had to raise up an individual who became a counter-cultural resistance to the spiritual decline of the day. To his generation, he was like that annoying, blaring alarm clock that insists on disturbing you from the comfort of your bed; you desperately want to stay asleep, but you know deep down that you need to wake up. John's lifestyle was constantly sounding an alarm to a culture that was deep in sleep, declaring that it was time to wake up!

The truth is that you don't know you're asleep until you wake up. Many times, God raises up people around us that are awake to him in ways we are not in order to break us free from our spiritual slumber. Because the nation was in an extreme place of dullness, darkness and compromise, God had to raise up someone on the other extreme of holiness, fire and devotion. This points to an underlying principle: when a nation is in its darkest hour, God will often raise up his greatest and most intense prophets. Moses, Elijah, Daniel and Jeremiah are just a few examples of this in Israel's history.

When we look across the nations of the world, it doesn't feel like an exaggeration to say that we are in the depths of our darkest hour in many ways; the rise of ideologies and political, socio-economic systems that are anti-Christ in nature, and the increase in immorality and perversion are clear indicators that all is not well. Certain lifestyles that were considered unacceptable by society only a few years ago are now accepted as the norm. Nations that were built on biblical foundations have turned around and are rejecting the very principles that made them great. Here we see the hearts of the children disconnected from the hearts of their fathers: the very opposite of one of the workings of the spirit of Elijah, as seen in Luke 1:17 (quoting Joel 2:28). It is in times like these that God raises up his greatest prophets. The enemy is behind this turning of the hearts of our generation away from the ancient paths of righteousness. The enemy has been busy turning the hearts of many from the hearts of their godly forefathers, whose sacrifice and obedience released God's blessings upon the land.

John the Baptist's intensity in his devotion to the Lord led to the advancing of the kingdom of God in his generation in a way that had never been seen before. Could it be that God, in his sovereignty, gave me and you an intense nature in order for us to be part of a counter-cultural resistance to the intensity of the kingdom of darkness in our generation?

It seems to me that the intensity of the darkness we are currently facing in our generation provides the perfect conditions for the raising up of the greatest and most intense prophetic movement the world has ever seen. In fact, the prophecy of Joel 2:28 and Luke 1:17, about the outpouring of the Spirit of God on all flesh and the release of the prophetic anointing *en masse*, comes in the context of great darkness. The enemy also knows the prophecy of Malachi:

> Behold, I will send you Elijah the prophet before the coming of the great and dreadful day of the Lord. And he will turn the hearts of the fathers to the children, and the hearts of the children to their fathers, lest I come and strike the earth with a curse.
>
> — Malachi 3:5–6

The disconnection between the hearts of the fathers and the children has resulted in a curse on the land, and Elijah is sent in order to prevent this.

The angel Gabriel called this to mind when he spoke to Zechariah about the calling of God on John's life, before John was conceived:

> He will also go before him in the spirit and power of Elijah, 'to turn the hearts of the fathers to the children,' and the disobedient to the wisdom of the just, to make ready a people prepared for the Lord.
> — Luke 1:17

It's worth noting that even though John carried the spirit of Elijah, we don't have records of any miracles he performed. Elijah is famous for some incredible miracles, such as the small matter of calling down fire from heaven! It is clear to me from examining the life of Elijah that his main thrust in ministry was seeing a nation turn back to God, and the great miracles he is famous for are mostly connected with this idea – seeing national spiritual awakening to Yahweh God. John the Baptist carried the same DNA in his ministry. Elijah raised the dead, physically, whereas John raised a nation from the dead, spiritually. So, even though John is not recorded as doing any miracles, the essence of his ministry was the same as that of Elijah.

After my encounter with the Lord on November 11, 2009, over time I became more aware of aspects of John's life and calling that are critical for those the Lord will use in these last days. Certain traits give us an insight into what it means to live a life on fire for the Lord that results in transformation in a nation. I'm sure this is not an exhaustive list, but here are a few I want to highlight:

1. HE WAS CALLED TO BE GREAT IN THE SIGHT OF THE LORD

> For he will be great in the sight of the Lord, and shall drink neither wine nor strong drink. He will also be filled with the Holy Spirit, even from his mother's womb.
>
> — Luke 1:15

The angel Gabriel told Zechariah that John would be great in the sight of the Lord. Note that he didn't say John would be great in the sight of man. Even though John was great in the sight of man, his primary calling was to be great in God's eyes. It is possible to be great in the sight of the Lord and not great in the sight of man. It is also possible to be great in the sight of man and not great in the sight of the Lord. Which would you choose? We so often gravitate towards the things that will make us look great to the people around us, and while being great in the sight of man is not wrong in itself, it becomes a problem when we let it define our identity and sense of worth.

Our priority in life should be greatness in the sight of the Lord. This means that we invest our lives in what is 'not seen' and often despised by man – things like prayer and devotion. I believe that what made John great in the sight of the Lord was his secret life of prayer and fasting. This was the foundation on which God could raise him up to be 'a voice' that brought about national transformation. Now, there are times when being great in the sight of the Lord would also lead us to being great in the sight of man, but we have to be ready for the fact that this is not always the case. Breaking and remaining free from spiritual slumber requires that we become individuals who have a primary focus on being great in the sight of the Lord.

2. HE LIVED IN THE DESERT

The desert was the process through which God shaped and equipped John to be a voice that prepares the way of the Lord. Desert conditions are not easy on the flesh, but they are necessary for raising up prophetic voices that bring about national transformation. God will often use the desert place to refine, purge and awaken the ones that he has called to bring an awakening, to be a voice that wakes others from slumber.

Moses was in the desert for 40 years before he was commissioned to lead the nation of Israel out of captivity; the apostle Paul was in the desert for three years after his conversion, being instructed by the Holy Spirit in the ways of God; and finally, John the Baptist was in the desert for many years until the day of his manifestation to Israel. It seems to me that some of God's greatest prophets are forged in the uncomfortable solitude of desert places, including the so-called 'Desert Fathers and Mothers', who set the pattern of radical devotional and cultural transformation that is reflected in the monastic communities of St Benedict and St Francis.

John was in the desert but the desert was not in John. Luke writes about him, 'So the child grew and became strong in spirit, and was in the desert till the day of his manifestation to Israel.' (1:80). In John 5:35, Jesus says he was a burning and a shining lamp; even though, externally, John was in a dry place, on the inside he was on fire.

3. HE WAS STRONG IN SPIRIT

Like Elijah, John was a man of great spiritual stature and stamina. It would have been impossible for him to fulfil the calling of God on his life without spiritual stamina. God had to take him to the spiritual gym, where he learned to exercise and build up his spiritual muscles. The Bible says, in Luke 1:80, that John grew 'strong in spirit.' Growing strong does not happen overnight. He had to consistently engage in certain spiritual activities, over a period of time, and his spiritual stamina gradually increased. Despite very little experience of

going to the gym, I do know that in order to build bigger
muscles you need to lift heavier weights, lift them regularly
and lift them consistently. Growing in strength involves effort
and pain!

There are two things we must hang onto here: consistency in spiritual discipline and embracing pain as part of
the process. God is looking to raise a generation of believers
who are consistent in seeking his face. In fact, we will not
grow strong in spirit without regular face time with God, in
communion and deep fellowship. There are no shortcuts to
growing strong in spirit.

Secondly, embracing pain means accepting that there will
be trials and tribulations. These days, there is a version of the
gospel that would have us believe that once we give our lives
to Jesus, he just gives us everything we want and we can sit
back and enjoy an easy life. So we see many people come to
Jesus with a consumer mindset, treating him like the genie
of the lamp, who's just there to grant all their wishes. Now,
don't get me wrong: God is a good father and he does want
to meet our needs. He himself tells us to ask, seek and knock
(Matthew 7:7). But the question to ask ourselves is this: does
God exist for us or do we exist for him? I love how Tim Keller,
a Christian apologist, theologian and pastor puts it: 'Trials
reveal your motivations in the faith: Am I serving God or do
I want God to serve me?' I believe that going through trials
is a significant and necessary part of the process of growing
strong in spirit.

If we are going to be people that prepare the way, we too must be strong in spirit. To be strong in spirit, we must be consistent in our spiritual disciplines and embrace the trials as a means of developing spiritual stamina. In the book of James, we are encouraged as believers to 'count it all joy' when we fall into trials:

> My brethren, count it all joy when you fall into various trials, knowing that the testing of your faith produces patience. But let patience have its perfect work, that you may be perfect and complete, lacking nothing.
>
> — James 1:2–4

I don't know about you but I find this enormously challenging. When I'm in the middle of a trial, the last thing on my mind is to 'count it all joy'. But as I look back on my life I realise that significant gains in my spiritual development have often come as a result of difficult and testing circumstances. What James is saying here is that the challenges we experience in our lives are an essential part of spiritual maturity.

4. HE HAD TO BE PREPARED

In order to prepare the way of the Lord, John himself had to be prepared. The supernatural events surrounding his conception did not exempt him from having to pass through the process of preparation for the manifestation of the fullness of the calling of God in his life. And his preparation took many years. We live in a generation that struggles to wait. We want everything fast, everything now! This means we often fail to understand the ways of God and get frustrated when we are not, right now, seeing a full manifestation of everything the Lord has promised. In the book of Hebrews, we read this:

> For you have need of endurance, so that after you have
> done the will of God, you may receive the promise.
>   — Hebrews 10:36

The promise cannot be received without endurance. Doing the will of God is one thing; receiving the promise is quite another. So it appears that it is possible to do the will of God and still not receive the promise – all because of a lack of endurance. I guess this is kind of important then!

Imagine if every time we did the will of God, we all received an instant reward. I think everyone would be doing the will of God all the time! Endurance is necessary after doing the will of God because, often, we don't see an instant manifestation of the promise.

John the Baptist developed endurance over the course of those many years in the desert, when he was being prepared by the Lord for a day of manifestation to Israel. The fact that God shows us what he has called us to do, does not always mean we are immediately ready to do it. In fact, many times, God will delay in releasing the very things he has for us because he knows that if we receive them prematurely, they will destroy us. The people of God, called to prepare the way of the Lord, need to be prepared. Walking with God requires a great deal of patience and endurance.

5. HE WAS THE VOICE

> In those days John the Baptist came preaching in the wilderness of Judea, and saying, 'Repent, for the kingdom of heaven is at hand!' For this is he who was spoken of by the prophet Isaiah, saying: 'The voice of one crying in the wilderness: "Prepare the way of the Lord; Make his paths straight."'
>
> — Matthew 3:1–5

When John spoke, people came under a spirit of conviction. His ministry impacted the whole nation because he carried great spiritual authority, and this came as a direct consequence of his proximity to the heart of God. John invested a lot of time in seeking the face of God, and it's impossible to seek the face of God and miss his mouth. To be 'the voice' he had to first be 'an ear'; to be 'an ear' he had to be close to the heart of God. The impact that John's voice had in public was a manifestation of the depth and quality of his secret life in God. It is amazing, and very sad, that we tend to prioritise the desire to have an impact and an influence in the public arena, while neglecting the quality of our secret life in God. When we learn to seek the Lord's face, we cannot fail to hear what he has to say to us.

For the sake of integrity, and sustainability, we should focus more attention on the reality of our private walk with God than on our public reputation. Just like an iceberg, where more than 90% of its mass is hidden underwater, a greater portion of our relationship with God should be in the secret place of private fellowship with him. It is from this place that God is able to amplify our lives to have a lasting impact on our world. If we gain a greater voice in the public place and lose a hearing ear in the secret place, we will only amplify our failure in the secret place before the masses.

I love what Gordon MacDonald once said on this subject: 'We are naively inclined to believe that the most publicly active person is the most privately spiritual.' He captures the essence of a subtle form of deception that so easily creeps into many of our minds. Having been in full time ministry for over 13 years I know how easy it is to fall in love with the work of God, while neglecting the God of the work.

It is the quality of what goes on in private that determines the impact we have in public. John's voice to the masses did not come through self-promotion; he was supernaturally endorsed by heaven. He was 'the voice', not 'the echo' – he wasn't just repeating what he had heard from someone else. He paid the price to get close enough to God to hear his whispers and feel his passion. John was a man of prayer and fasting. He didn't just preach a message; he was the message. His lifestyle embodied the message he carried. The lifestyle of the messenger must convey the weightiness of the message, otherwise they are not a voice but an echo. I believe the Lord wants us not just to preach a message but to be the message.

In the Introduction, I shared about how God had used Lou Engle to deeply impact my life. Over the last few years, I have been privileged to spend time with him and his family in various situations and I always leave deeply impacted. I often come back home to my wife saying 'Wow! He's not just on fire when he's preaching on a platform, he is literally the embodiment of what he preaches.' To me, Lou Engle is a great example of a person who has become the very message he has been commissioned by heaven to preach. Do you want to be a voice or do you want to be an echo?

So what does a 21st century version of John the Baptist look like? This is a question I have asked the Lord many times over the years. The challenges we are facing in our generation are very different to the challenges that John faced in his, so it's important to contextualise the calling to be forerunners like John in preparing the way for Jesus' second coming. We may be living in different times, but the principles and values that shaped the way John lived should call out across the centuries and challenge us today.

ELIJAH IS COMING... IN US

In Matthew 17 we read about Jesus going up a high mountain with three of his disciples – Peter, James and John. On this mountain, something pretty unusual took place: Jesus was transfigured before their eyes! His clothes became as white as light and his face shone like the sun. As if that wasn't enough, Moses and Elijah appeared alongside him, and he was in conversation with them as his disciples looked on, utterly amazed.

Elijah and Moses are two of the most significant prophets in the Bible. They both had incredible walks with God. Moses died and was buried by God (Deuteronomy 34:5-6), while Elijah was physically taken up into heaven by a whirlwind and didn't experience death (2 Kings 2:1)! So, you can imagine how mind blowing it must have been for Peter, James and John to see both Moses and Elijah talking with Jesus, right in front of them. The following passage records the conversation between Jesus and his disciples, immediately after this incredible experience:

> Now as they came down from the mountain, Jesus commanded them, saying, 'Tell the vision to no one until the Son of Man is risen from the dead.' And his disciples asked him, saying, 'Why then do the scribes say that Elijah must come first?' Jesus answered and said to them, 'Indeed, Elijah is coming first and will restore all things. But I say to you that Elijah has come already, and they did not know him but did to him whatever they wished. Likewise the Son of Man is also about to suffer at their hands.' Then the disciples understood that he spoke to them of John the Baptist.
> — Matthew 17:10–13

Jesus starts by warning Peter, James and John not to tell the vision to anyone until he is risen from the dead. This secrecy must have confused the disciples because, according to traditional Jewish eschatology, Elijah was due to come first, before the appearance of the Messiah (Malachi 4:5-6). They had just seen Elijah on the mountain top and were probably more convinced than ever that Jesus must be the Messiah.

It is also possible that the teachers of the law had used this same argument as 'proof' that Jesus could not be the promised Messiah, because Elijah hadn't yet appeared. So the disciples were probably thinking, at this point, that it would be a good idea to get the word out that they had just seen Elijah, because it would help to convince many more people that Jesus was, in fact, the Messiah. Puzzled by Jesus' command to keep it quiet, the disciples ask an important question: 'Why then do the scribes say that Elijah must come first?'

Jesus' response is very interesting. Firstly, he validates the teaching of the scribes by saying, 'Indeed, Elijah is coming first and will restore all things' but he then goes on to say, 'Elijah has come already, and they did not know him but did to him whatever they wished' and the disciples understand him to be referring to John the Baptist. Some have taken this statement to mean that Elijah is not coming because he has already come in the person of John the Baptist, but this ignores Jesus' affirmation that, 'Indeed he [Elijah] is coming first and will restore all things.' I believe this confirms that we should expect a future manifestation, apart from John the Baptist.

How could Jesus say, on the one hand, 'Indeed he is coming' and then go on to say, 'Elijah has already come'? This seems like a contradiction, right? But I don't think it is when we understand that biblical prophecies sometimes carry different layers of meaning and fulfilment. For instance, in Acts 1:10, when Jesus was supernaturally lifted up into heaven 40 days after his resurrection, two angels appeared to the disciples saying, 'This same Jesus, who has been taken from you into heaven, will come back in the same way you have seen him go into heaven.' Also, in Matthew 18:20, Jesus says, 'For where two or three gather in my name, there am I with them.' And in Matthew 28:20, he says, '...surely I am with you always, to the very end of the age.' So, in a sense, we can say that Jesus is here with us when we gather in his name, but also that he is coming again. Both are absolutely true. He is here and he is coming. Another example of this can be found in John 4:23, where Jesus says:

> But the hour is *coming*, and *now is*, when the true worshippers will worship the Father in spirit and truth; for the Father is seeking such to worship him.
>
> — John 4:23 (emphasis added)

Well, is the hour coming or is it now? The answer is both: it is here and it is coming.

In a similar way, I understand Jesus to be saying that Elijah has come (referring to the person of John the Baptist) and Elijah is coming. When Jesus says, 'Elijah is coming', this could mean both the person of Elijah and the spirit of Elijah. I believe, as we get closer to the return of Christ, the spirit of Elijah will be released all over the earth. Just as the spirit of Elijah rested on John to prepare the way for the coming of Jesus, I believe the same spirit is going to rest upon a generation to prepare the way for Jesus' return. John the Baptist was a prototype of a new breed of believer that the Lord will raise up in these last days to prepare the way for his second coming.

The significance of the person for whom John was preparing the way demanded a certain depth of consecration in his lifestyle, which is another reason why he was unusually intense. This tells me that the spirit of Elijah resting upon a generation to prepare the way for the second coming of Jesus will cause this generation to be intense in their lifestyle, because the magnitude of what they are preparing the way for will demand an uncommon depth of consecration in every area of their lives. If John lived the way he did to prepare the way for the first coming of Jesus, what does that mean for those called to prepare the way for the second coming?

As I look back on my prophetic journey with 11:11, and God calling me to be a forerunner like John in fasting and prayer, I realise that God is doing this same thing across the whole earth. I have met many Christians, young and old, from different backgrounds, who have sensed a similar calling and a desire to be radical in devotion in their relationship with Jesus. They have sensed a craving for tenacity and intensity in their prayer life, and I believe this is one of the key manifestations of the spirit of Elijah upon the life of an individual. The spirit of Elijah is currently being released across the nations of the earth in preparation for the return of Jesus.

Just as it was with John, so it will be with the new breed of believers the Lord is raising up across the earth: individuals who have been awakened from spiritual slumber and complacency to a life of radical devotion to Jesus.

Do you sense a stirring in your heart as you read this? Perhaps the Lord is calling you to be a 21st century version of John the Baptist. Now, this doesn't mean you have to go into a physical desert place, eat locusts and wild honey, wear camel hair, and all that jazz. But the same principles that dictated the way that John lived in his day should shape the way we live today as we prepare for the return of Jesus.

John was a Levite and could have served as a priest in the temple, enjoying a comfortable lifestyle, but he chose to separate himself from the familiar and accepted religious culture of his day in order to be a voice of change, ushering in a new day and declaring, 'Behold! The Lamb of God that takes away the sins of the world.'

John was focused, he had tunnel vision. He knew his calling and he gave himself fully to it. Are you easily distracted by the fleeting pleasures of this world or are you wholehearted in your pursuit of a deeper relationship with the Lord? With so many things fighting for our attention, it is so easy to lose focus. Social media and entertainment are not, in and of themselves, bad but they are temporal pleasures of this world and too many of us are intoxicated by them. How does the amount of time you spend seeking God compare to the amount of time you spend scrolling your phone or streaming boxsets? Is fasting an important part of your spiritual life?

John was consecrated. This means he was holy and set apart for God. He wasn't flirting with sin or living in any form of compromise. He had no inward toleration for anything that was opposed to the standard of God. Holiness may not be a popular word on the earth, but it certainly is in heaven. John hated sin. Are you quick to expose, confess and repent of sinful thoughts and ways?

A LITTLE TOO LEGALISTIC?

When I talk about living radically in devotion to Jesus, I often hear people express concern about falling into legalism – in other words, being tied to the exact letter rather than the spirit of the law – and this is understandable.

I think there is a massive difference between functioning in our relationship with God *for his love*, and functioning in our relationship with God *from a place of love*. This might sound like a subtle distinction, but it has a huge impact on the quality and longevity of our spirituality. It's important to understand that God loves us all the same, whether we fast and pray or not! But the more of his love and presence we encounter, the more we desperately want to give ourselves to him. So my response in fasting and prayer should come from a place of complete confidence in his love for me, and a desire to seek more of him.

The Father said to Jesus, 'This is my Son, whom I love; with him I am well pleased' (Matthew 3:17) a long time before Jesus carried out any miracles, proving that the pleasure the Father had in Jesus was not based on his ability to 'perform' in ministry activities. The Father's pleasure in Jesus was based on the fact that Jesus was his son. Jesus' identity was rooted in the love of the Father. It was from this place of security that the Holy Spirit drove him into the desert to fast for 40 days! So Jesus was fasting from a place of love and acceptance, not in order to gain love and acceptance.

But still, it is worth noting that as an athlete prepares for a significant tournament, like the Olympics, they take a lot of time to focus, exercise and prepare their body and mind. I bet this process looks pretty strict and legalistic, too. Once a top athlete decides to participate in a competition, everything in their world becomes focused on winning. This focus means that they have to let go of a lot other distractions, and they have to adhere to a very strict diet and exercise routine. To one who doesn't share their passion for what they do, their vision and commitment to their goal may well seem a bit over the top and unnecessarily intense. But because they have a clear vision of what's ahead of them, it brings focus to every area of their lives. In the same way, I believe that the life of radical devotion to Jesus comes from a clear vision of the prize of the high calling of God in Christ Jesus. As Paul writes:

> I press toward the goal for the prize of the upward call
> of God in Christ Jesus.
>
> — Philippians 3:14

We need to press towards the mark. This requires effort, and also implies some level of resistance that we must push through. I have seen and I am seeing God raise up more young people across the nations of the earth who carry this heart and want to be used by him to usher in a great awakening – not because they want to make a name for themselves, but out of a desire to make his name great in all the earth!

Is your heart stirred to be part of this end time army that the Lord is raising up across the earth to prepare the way for his second coming? Do you want to be a forerunner, like John was in his generation? Why not pray this short prayer and make a commitment to the Lord right now:

Heavenly Father, thank you for the invitation to be a forerunner, like John was in his generation. I'm sorry for allowing the temporal pleasures of this world to distract me from the eternal pleasures of deep fellowship with you. I turn away from distraction, and from any sin I have tolerated in my life. I ask you for the grace to give myself wholeheartedly in love for you. Give me a tunnel vision, fixed on you. Set my heart on fire in a fresh way, Lord, and cause my desires to be aligned with yours. I ask this in Jesus' name. Amen.

CHAPTER TWO

SQUARING UP

Enter the fight you were born for

In the summer of 2007, I had just finished my final year of studying Audio Video Broadcast Engineering at the University of Salford. I was so excited and relieved to be free from the constant pressure of my dissertation deadline and preparing for final exams. But I wasn't quite sure what I was going to do next. Three years earlier, just before I started university, I had a strong desire to go to Bible school, but now that desire was completely gone. Many of my friends had started filling in applications for jobs and that seemed like the right next step. The only problem was that I also had no desire to spend hours applying for job after job – and this wasn't out of laziness. I just had a desire to spend more time seeking God.

I wasn't sure what God had for me in the future but I knew I wanted more of him. It was at this time that I said something to myself that made no earthly sense – it even seemed outright arrogant – but somehow I knew that it carried authority. I remember saying to myself, 'I will not apply for any jobs. The right job will come to me.' It still shocks me, even now, that I said those words and actually believed them! It wasn't just a 'positive confession', or something I said out of laziness. In hindsight, I realise that what I said was not just of the Lord but was, I think, a manifestation of the gift of faith (1 Corinthians 12:9). Faith is one of the gifts of spirit, where the Holy Spirit provides a believer with extraordinary confidence in God's promises. This should not be confused with saving faith (Ephesians 2:8-9), which is something possessed by all believers. At the time, I was living at home with my parents and had hardly any financial responsibilities. Since I wasn't spending all my time applying for jobs, I had more time to fast and pray, and that's exactly what I did. Not knowing what I was going to do next and seeing all my friends applying for jobs made me wonder what God was up to. Thankfully my parents were supportive of the way I was using my time. I don't actually remember sharing with them my conviction to not apply for any jobs, but I know they loved the fact that I was spending a lot of my time seeking God, so they weren't worried!

Several months later, I was offered a job at Trafford Council, and after a short period of working there I received another offer from The Message Trust to work as their prayer coordinator. Now, several years later, I look back on that experience and realise that God was at work in a special way. Let me be clear, though, that I would not encourage anyone who has just finished university or anyone in need of a job to do what I did, unless you know with complete confidence that God has spoken to you. I should also point out that there have been other times when I have desired certain things in life to happen, and made similar declarations, and nothing came of it because my declaration was not born of the Spirit; it was simply wishful thinking, and therefore it did not carry any authority to bring into manifestation whatever I had declared.

There are several individuals in scripture who had a huge impact in shaping the destiny of a nation through certain declarations they made. These individuals carried a great weight of spiritual authority over kings, rulers and nations. Elijah is definitely at the top of the list when I think of characters in scripture that God used to shift the course of nations through powerful declarations.

Elijah is one of the outstanding heroes of the Bible. His name literally means, 'My God is Yahweh' and in many ways this was the essence of his message. He is often regarded as a wilderness dweller, which makes a lot of sense when we look at the parallels in lifestyle between Elijah and John the Baptist. While we know a lot about John's history, very little is known about Elijah's. In the biblical narrative, he seems to suddenly appear on the scene and start making bold declarations. The Bible doesn't give us much insight into what he had been doing or what had been going on in his life before his appearance as a prophet to the nation of Israel. Not much is known about his family or his geographical origin.

Elijah's first appearance in scripture is in 1 Kings 17:1, when he made a bold declaration that shook the entire nation:

> And Elijah the Tishbite, of the inhabitants of Gilead, said to Ahab, 'As the Lord God of Israel lives, before whom I stand, there shall not be dew nor rain these years, except at my word.'
>
> — 1 Kings 17:1

When Elijah released his declaration, the spiritual atmosphere of the whole nation responded to his words. His pronouncement that 'there shall not be dew nor rain... except at my word' could be taken as a pretty presumptuous statement.

Note that he didn't say, 'except at the word of the Lord.' This points us to the fact that he had a revelation of the authority he carried over the nation, and he had complete confidence in that. God let none of Elijah's words fall to the ground, just as he had for the prophet Samuel (1 Samuel 3:19). I can't help but wonder why Elijah's words carried such authority. Thankfully, we find the answer to this in the New Testament when we look at what the Holy Spirit revealed about Elijah, through the apostle James:

> Elijah was a man with a nature like ours, and he
> prayed earnestly that it would not rain; and it did not
> rain on the land for three years and six months.
>
> — James 5:17

So Elijah prayed earnestly that it would not rain. That makes things a bit clearer! We are not given this insight in 1 Kings 17:1; instead, it simply states that Elijah released a declaration.

It is very clear from the text in James that Elijah was a man of intense prayer. We don't know how long he must have prayed for the heavens to be shut but I doubt it was a five minute job. In fact, I often wonder whether the way we see him pray for the heavens to give rain in 1 Kings 18:41-44 is an indication of how he must have prayed for the heavens to be shut.

Earnest prayer speaks of intensity and tenacity. Intensity is related to depth of feeling and emotional connection to what he was praying for, and tenacity speaks of persistence, his ability to not be moved by the passage of time. Elijah's declaration before King Ahab was preceded by a great deal of prayer. I think these two qualities of tenacity and intensity are often missing in our prayer lives. There is often very little heart in our prayers and we give up too easily.

If our own prayers don't move us, why should heaven be moved? This spirit of intercession that is so evident in the life of Elijah is what distinguishes him from other biblical characters. It's time for us to see a breaking off of a lack of prayer as we cry out to God for the spirit of grace and supplication.

The way that Elijah suddenly appears in the biblical narrative mirrors something interesting in the life of John the Baptist:

> So the child grew and became strong in spirit, and was
> in the deserts till the day of his manifestation to Israel.
> — Luke 1:80

John had a day of manifestation to Israel. Before this appointed day he was in the desert for many years, fasting and praying. Since John carried the spirit of Elijah, it his highly likely that John's time in the wilderness, being prepared for a day of manifestation to the nation, reflects the way Elijah was hidden in the wilderness for years, being prepared for his own day of manifestation to Israel.

Prophets like Elijah do not suddenly appear overnight; rather, they are forged in the deserts of fasting and prayer.

Often, we get excited about the anointing and power of God on the life of an individual and we want what they have, but we don't appreciate what they've been through to get there. I believe that Elijah spent years in the secret place, seeking God and being prepared for a unique moment in history when God was going to bring to light and amplify his life of secret devotion before the nation. Prior to a public manifestation, Elijah lived out the reality of a private devotion.

Here's a sobering question for all of us: if God were to amplify to the nation our secret life of devotion, as he did with Elijah and John, would there be a spiritual awakening across the land? What is the quality of your secret life before God? The essence of true revival is found when God has found a consecrated people whose lives he can amplify.

I am always intrigued about the story of Elijah before his day of manifestation to Israel, because I believe that in understanding his origins we will discover some keys to prepare us for the battles of these last days. It's time to square up and enter the fight we were born for. Just as the Lord raised Elijah, so the Lord is raising up across the nations of the earth certain prophetic intercessors, whose words will shift entire nations and demand the attention of governments, kings and queens. Many of these voices are in the 'wilderness' right now, being prepared for the day of their manifestation to the nations.

Often, we desire the prophetic mantle of Elijah but despise his burden in intercession for a lost and broken nation. His authority as a prophetic voice to the nation of Israel was directly connected to the weight of the burden he carried in intercession, and the depth of his prayer life. In fact, as we look through the scriptures, we see that all the effective prophetic voices were great intercessors. For, as intercessors they were the voice of man to God, and as prophets they were the voice of God to man.

Joel 2:28 talks about the prophetic anointing being released *en masse* as we get nearer to the return of Christ. The prophetic anointing was never supposed to be disconnected from the intercessory burden. These days, it seems that many want to prophesy but very few want to pray. The Lord spoke through Jeremiah about one of the signs of a true prophet – their ability to intercede:

> But if they are prophets, and if the word of the Lord is with them, let them now make intercession to the Lord of hosts, that the vessels which are left in the house of the Lord, in the house of the king of Judah, and at Jerusalem, do not go to Babylon.
>
> — Jeremiah 27:18

Elijah was a prophetic intercessor, who had been prepared by God in the secret place and burst onto the stage of history in a moment when the nation of Israel was in the darkest place it had ever been spiritually.

In Chapter 1 we looked at Matthew 17:11, where Jesus said, 'Elijah is coming first and will restore all things.' I believe the spirit of Elijah is being released upon a generation, right now, to prepare the way for the second coming of Jesus.

ELIJAH'S NEMESIS: JEZEBEL

Elijah had a lifelong nemesis, an arch-enemy, with whom he waged war: Jezebel. But who was she? Her name means 'Where is the Prince (Baal)' or 'The Prince (Baal) exists', refer-ring to her god: the Phoenician, Baal. However, in biblical

Hebrew, the name Jezebel means 'There is no nobility', which is believed to most likely be an intentional distortion of her name by the writer of Kings in order to show utter contempt and disgust for her actions and religion. She was a remarkably wicked woman, whose reign in Israel – along with Ahab – brought to a climax the practice of Baal worship, a spread of immorality across the culture, and the persecution and execution of the prophets of God. Jezebel married King Ahab of Israel and this union paved the way for an increased wickedness in the land. 1 Kings 16:30–31 makes it clear:

> Now Ahab the son of Omri did evil in the sight of the Lord, more than all who were before him. And it came to pass, as though it had been a trivial thing for him to walk in the sins of Jeroboam the son of Nebat, that he took as his wife Jezebel the daughter of Ethbaal, king of the Sidonians; and he went and served Baal and worshipped him. Then he set up an altar for Baal in the temple of Baal, which he had built in Samaria. And Ahab made a wooden image. Ahab did more to provoke the Lord God of Israel to anger than all the kings of Israel who were before him.
>
> — 1 Kings 16:30–31

Before Ahab came on the scene, Jeroboam's sin was seen as the height of wickedness because he led Israel into idolatry. All through the book of Kings, the sin of Jeroboam is a constant theme. After the reign of Solomon, the kingdom split: Jeroboam became king of the northern kingdom (Israel), and Rehoboam (Solomon's son) became king of the southern kingdom (Judah). The temple was in Judah (Rehoboam's territory), so in order to stop the people from going all the way to Jerusalem to worship, Jeroboam erected two golden calves (one in Dan and the other in Bethel). By doing this, Jeroboam initiated a fusion of belief systems between pagan religion and the people of God in a bid to replace the traditional worship of Yahweh in Jerusalem. This union eventually culminated in national Baal worship under the reign of Ahab and Jezebel.

Ahab's apostasy in making Baal worship the state religion can also be connected to an incident referred to by Joshua as the 'sin at Peor' (Joshua 22:17). The sin at Peor is centred around Balaam's advice to Balak. In his bid to defeat and destroy the Israelites, Balak hired Balaam to curse them. After trying several times and failing to release a curse over them – in fact, much to his frustration, they were all the more blessed – Balaam devised a plan to cause Israel to forfeit God's protection.

The plan was to have the Moabite women invite the Israelite men to their fertility festival, which involved Baal worship and sex with temple prostitutes. This incident, recorded in Numbers 25, is the first mention of Baal in the Hebrew Bible. The enemy could not destroy them from the outside so the strategy was to 'become one' with them in sexual union, thereby causing them to lose God's protection and become the agents of their own destruction. All this to say that when Ahab chose to take Jezebel as his wife, this was essentially the sin at Peor being amplified and given a seal of approval by the highest levels of government.

Ahab didn't step into full-blown Baal worship until he married Jezebel. There was something about the union that amplified the seed of perversion that already existed in his heart. Jezebel was able to embody and execute to the full that which had already been accepted in the culture. She became the figurehead of the Baal worship religion. When God wanted to bring about a cultural revolution, he had to first challenge what the people in the culture had come to accept as normal.

Elijah's first declaration that 'there shall be no rain except at my word' was a direct challenge to Baal because the people saw Baal as the god of rain. By shutting the heavens, Elijah was showing the nation of Israel who the real God is. Baal was the god of the Canaanites, the god of fertility and the god that brought forth rain. They had sex orgies to call down the rain; they had prostitution in their religious institutions and in the worship of Baal; they offered up babies on demonic altars; and they sacrificed the blood of their sons and daughters (we will explore this in more detail in Chapter 6).

Ahab built an altar and temple for Baal in Samaria and had 450 prophets servicing this temple, while Jezebel housed the 400 prophets of Asherah in a sanctuary she built for them. Asherah was a fertility goddess of the sea, while Baal was the chief male deity of the Canaanites. Together, Baal and Asherah symbolise a demonic union, a wicked covenant, orchestrated by the devil for the purpose of reproducing deception and perversion across the land. This union had a physical manifestation in the marriage of Ahab and Jezebel.

THE SPIRIT OF JEZEBEL

You may have heard the phrase 'spirit of Jezebel'. This wording is not explicitly found in the Bible, but the essence of what this expression refers to is clear in scripture. I think it's important to understand that Queen Jezebel of the Old Testament was a physical embodiment of the attributes and characteristics of a very wicked spirit that existed long before she was born. In the book of Jeremiah, we read about the children of Israel worshipping the 'Queen of Heaven', a title that refers to an Assyrian and Babylonian goddess, also called Asherah, Hera or Astarte by other cultures and groups. Jezebel's father, Ethbaal, was both king of Sidon and a high priest of Baal, a consort of Asherah. Baal and Asherah worship go hand-in-hand.

Now, as a worshipper of Baal, Jezebel's whole life gave ultimate expression in the physical realm to the spirit that she worshipped. Today, when we refer to the 'spirit of Jezebel' we are not just referring to a human individual, we are actually referring an ancient spirit that has been called by several names over the centuries. The person of Jezebel was killed in 2 Kings 9, but the spirit that she embodied existed and functioned under various names before the person of Jezebel was even born, and that spirit still continues to function today (and it was clearly at play in the church of Thyatira, in Revelation 2:18–29).

The spirit of Jezebel is a principality that rules over nations, regions and people groups. According to Ephesians 6, evil spirit beings have rankings, leagues and a certain degree of functional order in the kingdom of darkness. Satan cannot be in two places at once and the same applies to principalities that serve directly under Satan. So in order to influence vast territories, a principality (such as a Jezebel spirit) will impart its nature into lower ranking demons and unclean spirits, who would then have the assignment of manifesting the very nature of the Jezebel spirit through individuals, media, churches, regions and nations. The spirit of Jezebel is, in essence, a spirit of seduction (more on this later).

Whenever the spirit of Jezebel is talked about, people are often too quick to think about someone they know – usually a woman – who they think carries this spirit. But a spirit of suspicion is not the same as a spirit of discernment! We have to be very careful when using labels like 'Jezebel' on specific people. For example, women with strong leadership abilities or strong personalities, but maybe lacking certain people skills, are not necessarily 'Jezebels'. The focus of this book is not so much about trying to identify a person who carries the spirit of Jezebel as it is about exposing the workings of this spirit in our society today. It is important to be clear that the spirit of Jezebel works through both men and women – in fact, I think more men carry this spirit than we realise.

I love what Mike Bickle (founder of the International House of Prayer, Kansas City) once said about this:

> A lot of people think about Jezebel and think of a woman with a strong personality. If her leadership is stronger than yours and you are a man, she is a Jezebel. The people most engaged in the spirit of Jezebel are men. They are the ones who are producing it, they are promoting it, they are partaking of it even more than women are...I have watched, over the years, a lot of women getting written off as a Jezebel spirit because their personality is strong. Again, they just need to get a few rough edges as well as their personality skills refined. A lot of guys have the same problem and nobody says 'Jezebel' to them. We are missing the whole thing because this is not the essence of what the spirit of Jezebel even is.*

The spirit of Jezebel is alive and well today, and I believe the Lord is raising a prophetic army that will destroy the influence of this spirit over our generation. The battle that started between Elijah and Jezebel thousands of years ago still rages on.

Elijah was opposed to everything that Jezebel represented. Elijah stood for purity, while Jezebel stood for perversion;

---

* Mike Bickle, *The Seven Churches in Revelation 2–3, Session 5: Jesus' Message to the Church of Thyatira* (mikebickle.org)

Elijah was for the preservation of life, while Jezebel was for the killing of babies; Elijah was zealous against wickedness, while Jezebel was zealous against righteousness; Elijah called for repentance, while Jezebel called for rebellion; Elijah was full of the words of God and truth, while Jezebel was full of witchcraft and deceit.

Elijah didn't start out by challenging Jezebel. Elijah was after a cultural revolution. The people had been far from the true worship of God long before Jezebel showed up. In order for there to be a true revolution, the heart of the people must be turned back to God. Elijah was in a fight for the soul of the nation.

Remember Jesus' words in Matthew 17:11: 'Elijah is coming'. If the spirit of Elijah is being released over a generation to prepare the way for the second coming of Jesus then, if we pay attention to the pattern of scripture, it is clear that the spirit of Jezebel will also be released over a generation by the enemy as a direct opposition and resistance to the spirit of Elijah. The battle between these two adversaries started in the days of Elijah and, hundreds of years later, it continued in the days of John the Baptist. As we near the return of Jesus, this battle will reach its most intense and climactic phase yet.

We are beginning to see the signs of this in our society today. As the body of Christ we must perceive and understand what is really behind certain trends, behavioural patterns and ideologies that many in our society (including some churches) have come to accept as normal. There's an age-old war raging between the spirit of Elijah and the spirit of Jezebel in our generation. It's a battle for the soul of our nation and generation. I believe it is time for us, the people of God, to square up for the fight of our lives.

Just like Elijah, we are called to see our nation turn back to God. Elijah's calling was rooted in a deep history of secret devotion to the Lord. Do you desire to see transformation on a national scale? Once again, would the amplification of your secret life of devotion to God result in transformation in the nation? Spiritual awakenings that result in national transformation never start in the public place; rather, they are born in the secret place of deep devotion to God.

We started this chapter by looking at the incredible authority Elijah held in the declaration he released to King Ahab. I believe God is still in the business of raising up prophets in the mould of Elijah, whose decrees and declarations over their nations will cause governments and rulers to pay full attention to what the Lord is doing and saying.

Elijah was building a secret history with God, until the day God decided to amplify his voice for the sake of shaking a nation out of the compromise of Baal worship. Do you have a secret history with God? Like any relationship, it does take time to build this kind of foundation, but the best time to start is right now. It's not too late! Spending regular quality time in his presence, through prayer and God's word, is a great starting point.

CHAPTER THREE

SHAPING UP

The path to purity is intimacy with God

I have been involved in the prayer movement here in the UK
for over 11 years. The ministry I lead, Prayer Storm, was
founded in 2009. I never really thought of myself as a prayer
leader, or even ever considered being involved in the prayer
movement in the way I have been for all these years. I feel like
I stumbled into this ministry. It wasn't really my plan, but it
was God's plan. In the early days, as I started to spend time
seeking God in fasting and prayer, I sensed his heart for the
youth of the nation. However, I found that a lot of the prayer
meetings I was connected with were almost entirely made up
of women – where were the men and the young people? This
bothered me.

With Joel 2:28 ringing in my ears ('…I will pour out my
Spirit on all flesh. Your sons and daughters will prophesy…'),

I felt the youth had to have a key role to play in preparing the way, in prayer, for the outpouring of God's Spirit on all flesh. So I started a weekly prayer meeting, and encouraged some of my friends to do the same. Eventually, these small prayer groups evolved into Prayer Storm: regional and national gatherings of fasting and prayer for the UK, all night prayer meetings, prayer and worship schools, and the list goes on.

In 2016 I found myself praying an unusual prayer (I don't remember ever praying this way before). I was asking the Lord to show me what we are really up against in our generation; I was praying for an increase in the spirit of discernment. I asked him to open my eyes to the reality of the opposition facing our generation in birthing his purposes in the earth. I don't think I really knew what this fully meant, I just wanted God to give me some insight through a revelation so that I could be more strategic and effective in our intercessory prayers. I must have prayed this for several weeks.

On the night of February 5, 2016, the Lord gave me a dream. I was in a large room, and there were a few people dotted around, chatting and socialising. My attention was drawn to one of the walls in this room that appeared to be covered in some kind of cloth. It was subtle and blended in with the colour of the other walls, but I knew instinctively to pull off the covering. It was as though I knew something was underneath the sheet that I needed to see. When I pulled off the covering, I saw that the wall underneath had all kinds of idols on it, from top to bottom. These idols were all carved images; they looked shiny but felt dark. Some looked like representations of Eastern religions, others were gods from Greek mythology. There were quite a lot of depictions on the wall that I did not recognise at all. All of a sudden, my attention was drawn to one of these idols that seemed to be alive; it was exuding such a strong aura that I found it terrifying. At this point in the dream, I was in two states: I was both in my body, and at the same time I was out of my body, observing the whole scene from above. It seemed like I was looking down at myself from the ceiling in that strange way that sometimes happens in dreams. I'd turned around so that my back was to the wall, but I was about 10 feet away from it. The idol that was emanating this awful power was behind me, on my right hand side.

I recognised the idol as the head of Medusa. Medusa is one of the most well-known figures from Greek mythology. She is depicted as a female, with a beautiful face, but with living venomous snakes for hair. According to the myth, anyone who looks at Medusa is turned to stone. At this time in my life, I didn't know much about Greek mythology, but in the dream I was certainly very conscious that I shouldn't make eye contact. I also felt a strong desire to cut the head off the wall, but with my back to it and taking care to avoid any eye contact, this was proving very challenging.

With every movement or attempt I made to cut off the head, it felt like its power increased all the more, and I could feel the intensity of its gaze pressing heavily on my back. The more I tried, the heavier it got, almost to the point where I couldn't stand up straight. To add to my frustration, I realised

I didn't have a sword in my hand. This didn't seem to stop me though, as I was determined to cut the head of Medusa off the wall, whatever it took. So I kept trying to move backwards, but with every movement it felt like I was being overpowered. The dream carried on like this for some time, until I eventually woke up. The time was probably around 5am, and I woke with the intense feeling of frustration that I had been experiencing in the dream. I quickly went into focused prayer.

I knew God was answering my constant prayer of the last several weeks and was now giving me a revelation into one of the main principalities opposing this generation. I wasn't exactly sure what the dream meant at the time, but I felt a very real disappointment and frustration that I hadn't succeeded in cutting Medusa's head off the wall.

DREAMS AND DISCERNMENT

At this point, I would like to highlight the importance of dreams. Many Christians don't take their dreams seriously, but it is very clear from scripture that God speaks through dreams! Reading through the account of Jesus' birth in the book of Matthew, it is amazing to me how many times God released specific instructions through dreams, and these revelations proved to be absolutely critical for Jesus' safety as a baby. Let's take a look at five instances where dreams shifted the trajectory of Joseph's life, and the lives of the wise men.

In Mary and Joseph's day, to be betrothed to someone was almost as though you were already married. It was a covenant between the couple. The only difference is that, in Jewish culture at the time, the consummation of the marriage would take place about a year after the betrothal. Mary was betrothed to Joseph and it was during this one year period that Mary had a visitation from the angel Gabriel and became pregnant with Jesus by the Holy Spirit. Just imagine how terrifying, awkward and embarrassing it must have been for Mary to explain this to Joseph. Understandably, Joseph was very upset by this news. He started planning to divorce Mary in secret, on the grounds of infidelity, so as not to make a public spectacle of her. The only thing that stopped him from going ahead with his plan was a dream:

> But while he thought about these things, behold, an angel of the Lord appeared to him in a dream, saying, 'Joseph, son of David, do not be afraid to take Mary as your wife, for that which is conceived in her is of the Holy Spirit. And she will bring forth a son, and you shall call his name Jesus, for he will save his people from their sins.'
>
> — Matthew 1:20–21

Joseph takes this dream seriously, pays attention to the instruction from the angel and marries Mary.

After the birth of Jesus, wise men came to Jerusalem in search of the baby, in order to worship him. The news got

to King Herod that these men were seeking the king of the
Jews, who had just been born. Feeling threatened by this
news, Herod told the wise men to let him know once they
found the newborn king, and claimed he wanted to offer his
worship too. But Herod was deceptive, and his true intention
was to kill the baby Jesus. The wise men did find Jesus, and
presented their gifts and their worship to him, and the only
reason they didn't return to Herod with the news was because
of a warning they received in a dream:

> And when they had come into the house, they saw
> the young child with Mary his mother, and fell down
> and worshipped him. And when they had opened their
> treasures, they presented gifts to him: gold, frankin-
> cense, and myrrh. Then, being divinely warned in a
> dream that they should not return to Herod, they
> departed for their own country another way.
>
> — Matthew 2:11–12

When Herod realised he had been deceived by the wise men
he decided to kill all the babies that were two years and under,
in Jerusalem and its surrounding districts. Only through a
dream was Jesus delivered from this massacre:

> Now when they had departed, behold, an angel of the
> Lord appeared to Joseph in a dream, saying, 'Arise,
> take the young child and his mother, flee to Egypt, and

stay there until I bring you word; for Herod will seek
the young child to destroy him.

— Matthew 2:13

Joseph and Mary stayed in Egypt for some time, until Herod's
death. Then, once again through a dream, Joseph was commanded to go back to Israel. After arriving there, he received
further supernatural direction from the Lord:

> Now when Herod was dead, behold, an angel of the
> Lord appeared in a dream to Joseph in Egypt, saying,
> 'Arise, take the young child and his mother, and go
> to the land of Israel, for those who sought the young
> child's life are dead.
>
> — Matthew 2:19–20

> But when he heard that Archelaus was reigning over
> Judea instead of his father Herod, he was afraid to go
> there. And being warned by God in a dream, he turned
> aside into the region of Galilee.
>
> — Matthew 2:22

Isn't it remarkable how dreams played such a significant role
in Jesus' early life? These dreams were all a matter of life
and death. Imagine what would have happened if, like many
Christians today, Joseph or the wise men hadn't taken their
dreams seriously.

The writer of Songs of Songs says this:

> I sleep, but my heart is awake.
>
> — Song of Songs 5:2

Even though our physical bodies are resting, our hearts can be awake to spiritual things. God often speaks to us in dreams, but it is also true that the enemy sometimes uses dreams to attack. When we sleep, our physical bodies rest but our spirit doesn't sleep; it is awake and open to receive communication from the spirit world.

This is one of the reasons why it is important that we invest in building up our spiritual strength by spending quality time in God's presence, through the word, worship and prayer. If you have a strong spirit, even when your physical body is asleep, your spirit is not only able to receive revelations from God but it is also able to resist and destroy works of darkness. I have personally experienced this several times. My understanding of the spirit world and its connection to my dream about the head of Medusa meant that when I woke up, I knew something was not right and I headed straight into prayer.

On the day of my dream, we were hosting a Prayer Storm meeting in Manchester. I was speaking at the conference, and we also had a guest speaker from London – Pastor Jonathan Oloyede – who leads the National Day of Prayer and Worship. While teaching on fasting (in preparation for a 40-day fast) I shared my dream, and Pastor Jonathan came up and said he felt that we all needed to go into a time of repentance for any form of inward toleration of immorality and sexual sin. So we took quite some time to repent and confess before God. We encouraged everyone at the conference to take part in this, whether or not they felt they were struggling with any form of sexual sin. Before this dream, I wasn't aware of any area of my life where I was tolerating immorality, but I knew it was very important that we all took part in this repentance together, asking God for a detox in our souls from the contaminations of the world. This simple yet powerful act brought about a massive shift in the meeting. The atmosphere completely changed. Many were on their knees in repentance, and others in tears and brokenness before the Lord. It was really powerful.

At the end of the conference, the most amazing thing happened. When we got home I turned on the TV and, to my surprise, right there on our TV screen was the thumb-nail for a movie that featured the very same head of Medusa I had seen in my dream that morning. However, this time the head had been successfully cut off and the guy who had cut it off was holding his sword in his hand! When my wife pointed this out to me, we were both in shock because we knew this was a confirmation, right before our eyes, of what had just taken place at the conference. I sensed that the Lord was also using this experience to show me that in order to cut off the head of Medusa – which, I believe, represented the spirit of Jezebel's influence in our generation – we first had to be cleansed through repentance from every inward toleration of this spirit. Without this, we could try and try again, as I had tried so desperately in my dream, but the idol would just become more and more powerful.

Over the years, as the Lord has continued to open my eyes and sharpen my discernment, I have become increasingly convinced that in these last days, as we near the return of Christ, one of the Church's greatest enemies – if not the greatest of them all – is this spirit of Jezebel. This book is not about demon hunting or magnifying the devil. It is about being forewarned and forearmed against the devices of the enemy.

I believe that what I saw in the dream was a manifestation of the spirit of Jezebel. The Lord was inviting me to a place of being cleansed of every inward toleration of this spirit so that I could exercise my authority in prayer to cut off its head. Even in my dream state, I had an instinctive awareness not to engage with its eyes. Now, I don't believe in Greek mythology but it seemed to me that God was using the imagery and reputation of Medusa to communicate to me the influence and power that the spirit of Jezebel has over our generation. Many believers have been turned to stone, so to speak, because they have allowed their eyes to engage with this spirit. Being turned to stone is a picture of neutralised authority.

It seems as if we are facing more darkness, perversion and addictions than any other generation in history. Our churches and many of our church leaders are infected by a system that we are called to affect. We, as the people of God, are in the world, but we can only truly change the world from a place of being different. Just like a boat, we can only stay on the water as long as the water does not get into the boat. Our problem is that we are letting the water get on top of us. We are losing our authority to change the world because many have been neutralised in authority through a willingness to compromise. You cannot have authority over an enemy that you're sleeping with.

We inadvertently try to replace authority with gifting, and we think our gifting can make up for what our compromise has cost us. We don't just need another gifted communicator, prophet, leader, singer or musician, who is able to move the souls of men but fails to cause the kingdom of darkness to tremble because of a lack of authentic authority. Elijah walked in authentic authority; when he spoke, the spirit realm recognised his voice. The level of darkness we are facing in our generation demands a new depth of purity in the hearts of God's people. We cannot be used by God to see nations turn to him if the principles of the worldly system remain comfortably at work in our souls, unchallenged.

HOW DO WE GET AUTHENTIC AUTHORITY?

In Psalm 24, David highlights the importance of purity when he writes about ascending the hill of the Lord:

> Who may ascend into the hill of the Lord?
> Or who may stand in his holy place?

> He who has clean hands and a pure heart,
> Who has not lifted up his soul to an idol,
> Nor sworn deceitfully.
>
> — Psalm 24:3–4

To ascend the hill of the Lord is to come to an elevated place of influence in the realm of the spirit. When we truly ascend the Lord's hill, we begin to operate in higher realms of authority. This is where God wants us as his children to operate from. However, the fact that it is God's desire for us to ascend his hill doesn't mean we are ready or able to just head on up there.

In these verses, I believe we see a road map for ascending the hill of the Lord. 'Who may stand in his holy place?' – this speaks of proximity in intimacy. We will not walk in authority if we are not rooted in intimacy with God. 'Clean hands and a pure heart' – this speaks of purity. The foundation of being a people who can be trusted to walk in uncommon realms of authority in God is purity of heart.

Simply put, the pathway to walking in an authority that will cause darkness to tremble is intimacy with God and purity of heart. We cannot exercise authority over the enemy if we are not rooted in intimacy with God, and we cannot remain in intimacy with God until we learn to walk in purity and exercise authority. As we draw near to God and grow in our intimacy with him, the enemy will make various attempts to distract us from the Lord. It is in times like these that we need to learn to exercise our authority and resist the devil from a posture of submission to God. If we don't do this, the activities of the enemy will eventually cause us to lose our intimacy with the Lord.

Jesus says that he has given us authority over all the powers of the enemy:

> 'Behold, I give you the authority to trample on serpents
> and scorpions, and over all the power of the enemy,
> and nothing shall by any means hurt you.'
> — Luke 10:19

It's interesting that he specifically refers to snakes and scorpions. Snakes and scorpions creep along the earth and we exercise authority over them by trampling on them. Is it possible that these two creatures in some way represent common manifestations of the works and influence of the enemy? I think so.

In 2 Corinthian 2:11 we are warned not to be ignorant of the devices of the enemy because, like these two creatures, the enemy is cunning, deceptive, seductive, poisonous and destructive. The great news is that we have been given authority over all the powers of the enemy. Our job is to exercise this authority by simply trampling. According to Ephesians 1 and 2, the enemy is under our feet because we are seated with Christ in heavenly places, far above all the powers of the enemy. So, anything that is meant to be under our feet should not be dominating our heads.

Even though, as believers in Christ, we are granted authority over all the powers of the enemy, we cannot exercise that authority effectively if there are any areas of our lives where we are in agreement with the darkness. I believe this is why I couldn't cut off the head of Medusa in my dream. Even though I wasn't consciously involved in anything immoral, my soul had to be cleansed of every subconscious toleration of the spirit of Jezebel. Until this cleansing had taken place, no true authority could be exercised over this spirit. The enemy has no authority except that which is handed to him by those who were given authority. As soon as we come into any form of agreement with the enemy we lose our authority over him. This is why repentance is so powerful. Through deep repentance at the prayer conference, the Lord was releasing our souls from the influence of this spirit of seduction. I believe this is what he was confirming to me when he gave me the sign of Medusa's decapitated head when I got home.

Are you reading this and thinking, 'How can I know true intimacy, authority and purity in my life?' One sure way to grow in these areas is to have regular 'heart checks' with the Lord. To understand what I mean by this, we'll need to take a look at a prayer of David from Psalms:

> Search me, O God, and know my heart: try me, and know my thoughts: And see if there be any wicked way in me, and lead me in the way everlasting.
>
> — Psalm 139:23–24 (KJV)

David is asking the Lord to search him because he knows we are limited in our ability to know the depths of our own hearts. There are certain things within you, things you don't know you possess or you don't realise you are capable of, because the circumstances that will trigger such things have not yet manifested in your life.

In 1 Corinthians 2:10 the apostle Paul tells us that the Spirit of God searches all things. So, in essence, the Holy Spirit is the deepest and most effective search engine there ever was, and ever will be. Far more powerful than Google! David is asking the Lord, through this incredible search engine of the person of the Holy Spirit, to expose his heart and his thoughts. Why? I think it is because David knew that purity of heart was of great importance if he was going to walk in deeper intimacy with the Lord, and therefore be able to exercise his authority in the earth. The sum total of the thought pattern that is sustained upon the heart of an individual is what defines who they really are. Solomon puts it this way: 'As a man thinks, so he is.' (Proverbs 23:7).

Reading through the Psalms, it appears that David knew the importance of having his heart searched by the Lord. This process of going through regular 'check-ups' with the Lord is so important, for several reasons, but let's look at one reason why examining our hearts and thoughts before God is critical for anyone wanting to grow in intimacy with him and walk in his authority.

After asking the Lord to search him and to try him, look at what David said next: 'See if there be any wicked way in me.' This simple yet profound prayer reveals that an individual who loves God and desires him could still have wickedness in their hearts and not even know it. If we don't do frequent hearts check with the Lord, we could become wicked in certain areas of our hearts and not even be aware of it. Some form of wickedness in our hearts is not always obvious to us, and that's why we need to regularly invite the Holy Spirit to search us and expose that which is impure, offensive or wicked in us.

I'm not talking about navel gazing and always living in a place of condemnation. No! I'm talking about allowing the Holy Spirit to expose anything that is hindering a deeper level of intimacy with him. I have heard it said many times that the Holy Spirit brings conviction, while the devil brings condemnation.

So what does this look like in practice? I believe it's as simple as praying with sincerity the same prayer that David prayed in Psalm 139:23–24, and then allowing the Holy Spirit to expose what needs to be exposed in your heart. As he does this, all you need to do is respond with repentance and obedience.

The Lord longs for his children to be holy, like he is holy, and one of the reasons for this is that we are his ambassadors on the earth. We are called to destroy the works of the enemy and advance God's kingdom. We will not be able to do this effectively if there are areas of our lives that the enemy has infiltrated. Purity of heart is the bedrock of an intimate walk with the Lord, where we can be effective in exercising authority on earth in advancing his kingdom.

PART TWO

RESISTING THE SPIRIT OF SEDUCTION

CHAPTER FOUR

EYES OF FIRE

Jesus and the spirit of Jezebel

A few years ago, I was invited to speak at a conference in London. The conference was taking place over a weekend, and I was scheduled to speak on the Friday and Saturday evenings. I arrived at my hotel in the afternoon and decided to spend some time praying. I have learned the importance of praying over hotel rooms and beds before I sleep. Let me digress a moment to explain.

In Genesis 27 we read about Jacob on the run from his brother Esau after deceiving their father Isaac in order to receive Esau's blessing. While on his way to Paddan-aram (his final destination), he stopped to sleep because it was getting late:

When he reached a certain place, he stopped for the night because the sun had set. Taking one of the stones there, he put it under his head and lay down to sleep. He had a dream in which he saw a stairway resting on the earth, with its top reaching to heaven, and the angels of God were ascending and descending on it ... When Jacob awoke from his sleep, he thought, 'Surely the Lord is in this place, and I was not aware of it.' He was afraid and said, 'How awesome is this place! This is none other than the house of God; this is the gate of heaven.'

— Genesis 28:11–12, 16–17

So, Jacob laid his head on a stone to sleep and had a dream that turned out to be a heavenly encounter. This encounter was based on the fact that Jacob's grandfather, Abraham, had built an altar in this very place (Bethel) many years before Jacob was born. Even though Jacob had no idea about what his grandfather had done in this place, that ignorance didn't stop him from having a spiritual experience when he laid his head on that stone. Basically, Jacob's encounter was a secondary consequence of what the person who was there before him had done – like a ripple effect. Is it possible that, just like Jacob, there are times when we lay our heads on a pillow in the physical realm without realising that we've placed them on an altar in the spirit realm?

Jacob's experience was a positive one, but I have had a few negative experiences when I have slept in certain places, and I have woken up knowing that my bad dream was connected to something that was done in that space before I got there. So, praying over hotel rooms and bedrooms has been something I have taken more seriously over the years, and I have found it to be very effective.

Now, back to the conference in London… When I arrived at the hotel, I spent some time praying; partly, I was praying over the room, as I've said, but I was also just spending some quality time with the Lord before the meeting that evening. Indeed, the meeting was very powerful, and I got back to my hotel room quite late and went straight to sleep. That night, I had a really interesting dream that felt a lot more like an experience in the spiritual realm.

In the dream, I was in the same hotel room and a lady walked in; someone I didn't know. She started talking to me about the things of God and was making references to scripture, so it seemed like the type of conversation I was used to having with fellow believers. However, there was one big problem: she was completely naked!

In the dream, I knew something wasn't right about this, but the lady just acted as though everything was fine. It actually reminded me of Revelation 2:20, where Jesus says that Jezebel teaches and seduces the servants of God. As she carried on talking to me I interrupted her and said sternly, 'You must leave.' Well, she didn't even acknowledge what I had said, so I repeated myself a second time, with even more conviction: 'You must leave!' Still no response. At this point I said, 'I take authority over you. You must leave now.'

Suddenly, she started to shake visibly, and she turned and ran out of the room. I ran after her and said, '…and I release the fire of God against you!' At that point, fire came out from me and hit her, and she disintegrated before my eyes. And that's when I woke up.

That night at the conference we stepped into a whole new level of breakthrough. When the church prayed, it felt as though every molecule in the room was charged; the atmosphere was electric, and something shifted over that church. I knew it was connected to the victory in my dream. Whenever I think of this experience, I am reminded of Jesus' words about Jezebel in Revelation, which we will come back to shortly. I am convinced that what I experienced was a manifestation of this spirit.

In the book of Revelation, Jesus addresses the seven churches with words that carry multiple layers of application. Firstly, it's worth noting that the letters were written to seven actual churches in John's generation, to address their spiritual condition and to encourage them in righteous living. Secondly, the letters were written for the benefit of all churches, both historical and present, with the aim of inspiring wholeheartedness in individuals. Lastly, the letters were written to prepare the Church as a whole for the end times, and the return of Christ.

What Jesus has to say to these churches gives us some incredible insights into how he considers our service to him and what he sees as most important. I believe that a regular review of what Jesus had to say about the seven churches is a good way for us to keep our hearts in check and maintain an eternal perspective in a world where it's so easy to get distracted by the here and now and lose sight of heaven's bigger picture. We should be more concerned about heaven's evaluation of our lives and service to God than about our reputation on earth.

There are a few common trends in Jesus' address to all seven churches. Firstly, he begins by highlighting a specific aspect of his majesty that each church needed to take hold of in order to overcome persecution or temptation. Secondly, he gives affirmations before he gives corrections (with the exceptions of Sardis and Laodicea, where no affirmations are given). Thirdly, Jesus gives corrections for compromise, exhorting the churches to specific responses, often with an element of warning. Lastly, he always promises a reward for those who overcome.

Following the dream I had at the hotel in London, I have been particularly intrigued by what Jesus had to say about the infamous character of Jezebel. So deep was the impact she had on the nation of Israel's spiritual life that, thousands of years later, Jesus makes reference to her in the book of Revelation:

> And to the angel of the church in Thyatira write, 'These things says the Son of God, who has eyes like a flame of fire, and his feet like fine brass: "I know your works, love, service, faith, and your patience; and as for your works, the last are more than the first. Nevertheless

> I have a few things against you, because you allow
> that woman Jezebel, who calls herself a prophetess, to
> teach and seduce my servants to commit sexual immo-
> rality and eat things sacrificed to idols.'"
>
> — Revelation 2:18–20

It is unclear whether Jesus was referring to an actual individual named Jezebel, or if he was using the name symboli-
cally. When we look at the historical reputation of the person
of Jezebel, and the feelings of disgust her name must have
sparked in the minds of many Jewish people, to me it would
be not just unfortunate but really shocking for someone to
have named their child Jezebel. I also find it hard to imagine
someone called Jezebel functioning in a New Testament
church, without choosing to change their name. All that to
say, I think it is highly unlikely this was a real person. Either
way, it doesn't really change the essence of the message Jesus
had for the church of Thyatira. We are now going to take
a closer look at Revelation 2:18-20, breaking down the
meaning of some of the things Jesus says about himself and
the spirit of Jezebel.

EYES LIKE A FLAME OF FIRE

Jesus' eyes are described as 'like a flame of fire.' This speaks of
his passion, his love, his holiness and his judgement. No one
can hide from those eyes. It is often said that the eyes are the

gateway to the soul. If Jesus' eyes are full of fire, I can only imagine that his heart must be ablaze! In other words, he is full of passion. This fire is good news for those whose hearts are yielded to him, those who are seeking to resist darkness in all its forms. To these he imparts his fire, which gives us passion for righteousness. His fiery eyes are also piercing eyes of judgement, to awaken and bring discipline and correction.

We tend to gravitate towards aspects of the nature of God that are easy to like, but I think it's important that we learn to embrace everything about his nature. The Bible gives a few definitive statements about who God is. For example, we often talk about the fact that God is love, and rightly so. Love is not just one of his attributes; it is the essence of who he is. Everything he does comes from the essence of who he is, the core of his character – Love. God doesn't just perform acts of love, he is love itself. But the fact that God is love is not in conflict with other aspects of his nature.

We also see in the Bible that God is light. God does not just produce light; he is light itself. He is not a type of light; his very character and nature is light. God is also a consuming fire: it is his nature. Obviously, fire is not God, but the essence of God is consuming fire. Fire is often used as a symbol of God and his judgement against sin. We cannot just embrace God's love and shy away from knowing him as a consuming fire. This results in a lack of fear of the Lord, a sort of complacency. Similarly, if we only embrace God as a consuming fire and ignore the fact that he is love, this leads to legalistic, judgemental Christianity.

The apostle John tells us that Jesus' eyes are on fire (Revelation 1:14); Ezekiel describes the being he saw on the throne as a being of fire (Ezekiel 1:27); Daniel tells us his throne is flaming fire, with wheels ablaze and a river of fire proceeding from it (Daniel 7:9-10); and Isaiah tells us the seraphim (also known as burning ones) fly around his throne (Isaiah 6:2). So, with Yahweh being on fire and everything around him being on fire, I think it is impossible for us to claim to be in close proximity to him and not be on fire. We were made to live a life on fire!

His eyes of fire are an invitation to live on fire in a cold and lukewarm world. To the church that is particularly struggling with the spirit of Jezebel, the revelation that he gives of himself begins with his fiery eyes. Why? Because once we catch a glimpse of the fire in his eyes, the witchcraft and seduction of Jezebel is broken off our lives. Fire is contagious. You cannot hang around the man of fire himself and not catch his fire. Once his fire becomes your fire, the spirit of Jezebel cannot keep you bound: the enemy cannot stand the fire of God! If we don't engage with Jesus' eyes of fire we will fall for Jezebel's eyes of seduction. Jesus was saying to the church of Thyatira, in short: 'You want to stay free from Jezebel? Then have a revelation of my burning eyes.'

FEET LIKE FINE BRASS

Jesus then goes on to talk about his feet being like fine brass or burnished bronze. This also represents his judgement against sin and his declaration to trample down all that is identified with Jezebel. In the previous chapter, we looked at Jesus' words in Luke 10:19 where he said, 'Behold, I give you the authority to trample on serpents and scorpions, and over all the power of the enemy, and nothing shall by any means hurt you.' The feet are used to exercise authority over the enemy. As a sign of victory, the enemy would often be trodden under foot. When Jezebel was killed, Jehu trampled her under his foot.

'I KNOW YOUR WORKS'

It's amazing what Jesus had to say about the 'works' of the Thyatira church. He affirms their ministry of love, service, faith and patience, and even goes on to say that they have grown in these areas: their love, service, faith and patience are more than when they started out. However, in spite of all this growth and effectiveness in ministry, as a church they are still being seduced into immorality and idolatry.

THE DIFFERENCE BETWEEN LOVE AND TOLERANCE

> Nevertheless I have a few things against you, because
> you allow that woman Jezebel, who calls herself a
> prophetess, to teach and seduce my servants to commit
> sexual immorality and eat things sacrificed to idols.
> — Revelation 2:20

The church of Thyatira allowed their commitment to love one another to outweigh their devotion to walk in holiness before the Lord as a community. The fact that Jesus said they tolerated Jezebel implies that they allowed this spirit to function in the church without challenging it. In the name of loving each other, they were allowing a spirit of seduction to function in their midst, unchallenged.

There is a false narrative of love and tolerance that has not just invaded Western society, but has sadly infected many of our churches too. For fear of being labelled as judgemental or unloving, many shy away from addressing ungodly behaviour in the life of a fellow Christian. Now, I am not implying that we should go around being bigots, criticising and calling out every wrong thing we see in the people around us. There is a right way of doing things in the Spirit. There is a time to speak the truth in love. Sadly, many want to 'love' but not speak the truth, while others err on the side of speaking the truth, but neglect to love.

The very spirit of Jezebel is seduction. Many of us are allowing seduction to go unchallenged in our lives. That is basically tolerating a spirit of Jezebel. To avoid tolerating this spirit, one has to speak up, because Jezebel dominates and wants to silence the people of God. We cannot allow a false narrative of love to stop us from speaking the truth in love.

SEXUAL IMMORALITY

Jesus' words to the church of Thyatira give us great insight into the workings of the spirit of Jezebel. It is true that the spirit of Jezebel in a church, business, family or community will often work through control, intimidation, manipulation, fear, spiritual pride... But at the core of the spirit of Jezebel is seduction and sexual immorality.

Jesus' address to the church of Thyatira is not just the longest to any of the seven churches, but it is also the only address in which he mentions sexual sin three times. On the first two occasions, he clearly speaks of sexual immorality, but the third time he makes reference to adultery, which is immorality. The only other church Jesus spoke to about sexual immorality was the church in Pergamos:

> But I have a few things against you, because you have
> there those who hold the doctrine of Balaam, who
> taught Balak to put a stumbling block before the

children of Israel, to eat things sacrificed to idols, and
to commit sexual immorality.

— Revelation 2:14

Balaam's advice to Balak involved using sexual immorality
as a means of getting the men of Israel to engage in their
fertility festival, which was Baal worship. As I said earlier,
it's worth remembering that what we call the Jezebel spirit
actually existed a long time before the person of Jezebel in 1
Kings was born. The spirit we call 'Jezebel' was the same spirit
that was at work when the men of Israel where seduced into
Baal worship through sexual immorality. So when Jesus talks
about what Balaam taught Balak, and the stumbling block
put before the children of Israel to commit sexual immorality,
I believe the same spirit that possessed Jezebel was at work
here – a spirit of seduction! This is at the heart of the workings
of the spirit of Jezebel.

'SHE CALLS HERSELF A PROPHETESS'

...who calls herself a prophetess, to teach and seduce
my servants to commit sexual immorality and eat
things sacrificed to idols.

— Revelation 2:20

Jesus' comment on this person is quite revealing. The fact
that she 'calls herself a prophetess' implies that Jesus doesn't

call her a prophetess. This should not in any way be taken as an indication of Jesus' disapproval of women prophets, as some have done. There are many examples of women, all through scripture, functioning as anointed prophets of God. This Jezebel was a self-proclaimed prophet.

In Chapter 1, we talked about John the Baptist being a voice of one crying out in the desert. An authentic voice does not come by self-promotion. Men and women anointed by God to fulfil an assignment in the earth do not need a title to function in their area of calling. Today, some leaders are more focused on having impressive-sounding titles than actually functioning in an anointing from God that effects change on the earth. This dysfunction stems from a place of misplaced identity and a need to be seen as important or significant.

The spirit of Jezebel exalts itself with 'spiritual giftings' in order to gain a position of influence. The fact that she had a following in the church implies that she could function in a way that gained her influence. This Jezebel could prophesy, but not by the Spirit of God. She could basically mimic the true gift of prophecy, so that the undiscerning were mesmerised and lured away into her web of deception. Jezebel may be able to mimic the move of the Spirit but she cannot mimic its holiness.

Some of Jesus' teachings in the Gospels very much affirm his words in Revelation. For example:

> By their fruits you shall know them.
>
> — Matthew 7:20

The church always gets into trouble when we start to idolise spiritual gifts (which can often be mimicked by the enemy). The gifts of the Spirit have got to match the fruit of the Spirit. There is a reason why we have nine gifts of the Spirit (1 Corinthians 12:1–11) and nine manifestations of the fruit of the Spirit (Galatians 5:22–23). Gifts of the Spirit in the life of a believer must be in line with the fruit of the Spirit in the life of that believer. You cannot fake fruit. The enemy can try to mimic fruit but he cannot produce fruit. Just as a mango tree does not have the ability to produce an orange, the enemy can never produce fruits of righteousness.

The fact that Jezebel was able to prophesy implies that she was operating from another source and not the Holy Spirit. Through familiar spirits, and a well networked kingdom of darkness, the spirit of Jezebel is able to release accurate words. What's important is not just the words that are being prophesied but where they are coming from. The source of the prophecy will determine the fruit it bears in the lives of the people that receive it. The slave girl heralding Paul and Silas in Acts 16:16-19 was very accurate in what she said, but was operating from a different source. Paul eventually had to confront the spirit she was operating under and cast it out.

> Nevertheless I have a few things against you, because you allow that woman Jezebel, who calls herself a prophetess, to teach and seduce my servants to commit sexual immorality and eat things sacrificed to idols.
>
> — Revelation 2:20

By calling herself a prophetess she was laying claim to divine revelation from God, and by teaching she was providing instruction to the church. Her influence over many in the church gave her a platform to teach, but the fruit of her teachings was sexual immorality in the lives of the people who came under her ministry. Her 'prophetic gift' de-sensitised her followers and prepared the way for them to receive her false teachings.

It is possible that this individual may have taught clearly and plainly that sexual immorality was okay and encouraged everyone to take part in immoral activities. However, I doubt this was the case. There was probably a lot more subtlety to the working of this person. I think it's telling that Jesus uses the word 'seduce'. To seduce is to mislead, to tempt, to draw into danger through attracting and deceiving. So I think her teachings would have had truth in them, but muddled in with deceptions, so what you have is a diluted message, a mixed message, coupled with the spirit behind the words.

> The words that I speak to you are spirit, and they are
> life.
> — John 6:63

Here, Jesus is saying: 'The words I speak to you carry spiritual substance that imparts life to the hearers and receivers of my words.' What made Jesus' words impart life? The Holy Spirit behind them.

I remember my wife, Rebecca, sharing with me about one of her teachers in primary school, who often told her, 'You will never accomplish anything.' Rebecca had no idea how deeply these words had impacted her until years later, when she realised that she was strangely unable to finish every major project she started. Thankfully, through prayer, this curse was broken over her. Words can carry either the presence of God or the presence of the devil, and they will impart either life or death.

The spirit behind the spoken word is revealed in the fruit produced in the lives of those receiving it. This person operating under the spirit of Jezebel in the church of Thyatira may not have explicitly taught in a way that encouraged everyone to take part in sexual immorality, but the fruit of her teachings in the lives of the believers was sexual immorality. Jesus warned us about wolves that dress in sheep's clothing:

> Beware of false prophets, who come to you in sheep's clothing, but inwardly they are ravenous wolves. You will know them by their fruits...
>
> — Matthew 7:15–16

There is a teaching on the grace of God that has grown in popularity in the Church, which pretty much says, 'Your past, present and future sins have been forgiven so you don't need to repent, because God's grace covers all your sins.' I believe this is a deception. The fruit of such teachings in the lives of believers is often carnality or worldliness, without repentance.

Any teaching on the grace of God that gives you liberty for carnality is heresy. I believe one of the ways to discern the spirit behind a teaching is to observe the fruit it bears in the lives of the individuals who receive it. God's grace does not make us free to sin, but free from sin. Jesus himself speaks to the churches in Revelation and tells them to repent. And these are Christians that he's talking to. For example:

> Remember therefore from where you have fallen; repent and do the first works, or else I will come to you quickly and remove your lampstand from its place – unless you repent.
>
> — Revelation 2:5

> Repent, or else I will come to you quickly and will fight against them with the sword of my mouth.
>
> — Revelation 2:16

> Indeed I will cast her into a sickbed, and those who commit adultery with her into great tribulation, unless they repent of their deeds.
>
> — Revelation 2:22

These are the words of Jesus and they are intense! He hates sin and expects us, his Church, to have a zero tolerance policy when it comes to sin. That's why he urges repentance. 1 John 1:9 says, 'If we confess our sins he is faithful and just to forgive us and to cleanse us from all unrighteousness.' The blood of Jesus does not cleanse in the dark. The blood of Jesus cleanses sins that are brought into the light, through confession. The fruit of accepting a false teaching on the grace of God is often to trivialise sin and repentance. In a similar way, the fruit of Jezebel's teachings in the Thyatiran church was seduction into sexual immorality.

The spirit of Jezebel uses 'spiritual gifts' to gain a position of influence and trust, and then begins to teach a diluted message to undiscerning hearts. In a secular environment, the spirit of Jezebel does not necessarily need to use spiritual gifts to gain a position of influence. It uses incredible natural abilities in the arts and entertainment, outstanding communication skills, musical abilities, administrative skills, etc. It really doesn't matter so much what the ability is, the strategy is still the same: gain a position of influence and then release teachings that seduce the masses into immorality. Again, I want to stress that the spirit of Jezebel is not just at work in women. It is a spirit, so it has no gender. It works through men and women just the same.

As I observe the different spheres of influence within culture, such as government, arts and entertainment, business, family, education and so on, it seems to me that there are ideologies being released that are clearly shaping our culture. Could the fruit that these ideologies produce in the lives of individuals give us insight into the spirit behind them? As we see an increase in sexual immorality, confusion and perversions like never before across our culture, could it be that there is a spirit influencing many in positions of power, leading them to release 'teachings' (i.e. laws, ideologies, entertainment, etc.) that seduce the masses into a lifestyle of deception, bondage and immorality?

I am not writing this to come against particular individuals and call them all Jezebels. My purpose is to expose a spirit at work that many are not aware of. 'Our wrestle is not against flesh and blood,' (Ephesians 6). We are engaged in a spiritual battle, and if we are to win we need spiritual weapons. The spirit of Jezebel is alive and well, throughout our culture.

What we have come to accept as normal in our 21st century Western culture was, only a few decades ago, considered abnormal and unacceptable. Our society has radically changed over the last few decades. In many ways, these changes have been monumental and exponential in their impact on our culture. They may at times have been gradual and subtle, but their impact has been huge, and there is a spiritual influence behind many of them. The fruit of these changes in the lives of individuals manifests the nature of the spirit behind them.

Previous generations gave the enemy a foothold by choosing compromise, and now the enemy has a stronghold in our culture. The compromise of one generation has led to the captivity of the next. Take, for instance, David and the sin of adultery with Bathsheba. One way of looking at this is that David had a weakness with women, but Solomon then took it to a whole new level: he had 700 wives and 300 concubines (1 Kings 11:3)! What started out as a compromise in David's life opened the door for that area of weakness to be amplified in the next generation. The compromises and sins we tolerate in our lives often become an area of captivity for our children.

It's not just affecting and infecting society, but it has also infected the Church. This is evident in the lifestyles of many multitudes across the world today. The agenda of Jezebel is to release Baal worship across culture, and Baal worship involves widespread sexual immorality.

Whether you have consciously tolerated this spirit in your life or have subconsciously been influenced by it, I think it is time to ask the Lord to expose every inward toleration to the spirit of Jezebel that we may have within us, repent for the times we have entertained this spirit in our lives, and ask him to give us a revelation of his burning eyes. Join me in this simple prayer:

Heavenly Father, let your light shine through every area of deception and darkness in my heart. Expose the works of the enemy, in and around me. I repent for where I have knowingly or unknowingly come into agreement with Jezebel. I break every agreement I may have entered into with this spirit, in the name of Jesus. Cleanse me of every inward toleration of the spirit of Jezebel by the blood of Jesus. Cause me to behold Jesus' eyes of fire and let them refine my emotions and desires. I ask for an increase in discernment in my life. Help me to see what you see and respond how you want me to respond. I pray this in Jesus' name. Amen!

CHAPTER FIVE

CLEANSED BY FIRE

Pursuing holiness in a Godless culture

My wife, Rebecca, has been involved in leading worship in church since she was a young child. It has been obvious to others that the hand of the Lord has been strong on her life, and I have been in meetings where I have observed that just the sound of her voice has brought freedom, deliverance and encounters with God to people in the room. I know there is such authority in her voice. But it wasn't always this way.

When Rebecca was a teenager she had an addiction to music and she would listen to almost anything she could get her hands on. She did try to stay away from music with bad language and music that she thought had blatantly negative elements to it, but she would always turn to music whenever she was having a bad time or needed an emotional boost.

Music became to her like fast food – it gives instant gratification but is ultimately bad for the body. She started to suspect that a lot of the secular music she listened to was dulling her senses to the things of the Holy Spirit, because she was so emotionally charged and connected to the music that she couldn't tell the difference between her emotional response to the music and the presence of God. She once sensed the Lord say to her, 'Every song has an assignment,' which she took to mean, in essence, that when we listen to songs we bring ourselves into alignment with the assignment (whether good or bad) of that music.

So the Holy Spirit started to convict her on what she was listening to. One day, she felt the Lord say to her, 'Am I worth giving this up for? Is my presence everything to you?' This led her to a place of brokenness and surrender to God. She would say that it took her two years to detox from all the dilution and pollution that had made its way into her through her addiction to secular music.

Everyone sings and writes according to the idols of their life. If you want to know the idols and ideologies of our generation then you can start by taking a look at the music charts. If we are sensitive to the Holy Spirit, sometimes we only need to hear the sound (not even the lyrics) to discern the spirit behind the song. Even without an acute sensitivity to the Holy Spirit in this way, hearing the lyrics and seeing some of the music videos for these songs should be enough to convince any committed Christian that the spirit behind them is demonic and that it promotes the culture of darkness.

This became even more obvious to us when Rebecca had an unusual dream. I want to tell you the dream and then interpret it for you. I believe it has an important message for what we're learning.

REBECCA'S PROPHETIC DREAM

In her dream, Rebecca was on one of the long main roads that runs through our city and across the nation, but the road was submerged under a big river. The river covered the entire stretch of this road and the city. She was in the river when all of a sudden she saw a mermaid swim past her, and at the same time she felt a real sense of fear and dread. The mermaid turned and started to swim towards her, smiling and projecting lust towards her, and pushing her backwards in the river. Suddenly, Rebecca found herself next to a house and she got out of the water, followed by the mermaid. As the mermaid stepped onto the pavement she turned into a human, a lone mother with a baby boy, who was very sick and dying. Rebecca looked at her and said, 'We need to repent of the mermaid spirit.' The more intense the repentance, the more the child was revived. He began to get stronger and was eventually completely healed as the mother repented.

In the next part of the dream, Rebecca found herself in our bedroom at home, but she had turned into Lou Engle (intercessor for revival and co-founder of TheCall) and was looking for some clothes. Instead, she pulled out a gold £1 coin, and on this coin was what looked like a woman wearing a war helmet, with a dress draped over her and her bare arms lifted up. Around both her arms was wrapped a giant snake. As this went on, she kept hearing this scripture repeated, over and over:

> I will give you the treasures of darkness, and hidden riches of secret places.
>
> — Isaiah 43:3

How did we interpret this strange dream? Mermaids are often known as sirens. They are usually portrayed as a beautiful woman from the waist up and a fish from the waist down. They are known for their enchanting songs and voices, which they can use to hypnotise, control and lure people to their death. I believe the first part of Rebecca's dream was a picture of the season of her life when she was addicted to music. The sound and emotions from the systems of the world and the kingdom of darkness were being projected to her and she was putting up no resistance. In fact, the sound from the mermaid or siren actually influenced her own sound.

If a believer doesn't take a conscious stand against darkness and perversion in the culture and climate we live in, they will be subconsciously influenced by it. By default, if you do not resist the enemy's projections by pressing in to God (which, by the way, will make you counter cultural) you backslide and lose ground. According to the word the Lord spoke to Rebecca, 'every song has an assignment,' and the assignment of the mermaid's song is death. All those who come under her influence are eventually lured to their death.

In the dream, Rebecca also represented some elements of the prophetic worship movement in the Church today, which is being contaminated by the sound of the enemy because of a lack of consecration. I believe the mermaid spirit in Rebecca's dream is also one of the manifestations of the spirit of Jezebel. Because of her mixed and muddled sound, the mermaid was not just able to project lust but was also now able to change Rebecca's direction. Here's how I interpret this.

I have come to believe that the spirit of Jezebel is the one of the main influences behind the secular music industry. Many popular male and female artists originated in the Church and then moved away as they found fame. To use the imagery of Rebecca's dream, they started out in the river but the spirit of Jezebel has taken them out and infiltrated their sound. If Jezebel can't take you out of the Church, she will infiltrate your sound to neutralise your authority and bring confusion and death to the prophetic worship in the Church.

When they got out of the river, the mermaid turned into a mother with a dying baby. This part of the dream calls to mind what Jesus says about the spirit of Jezebel:

> And I gave her time to repent of her sexual immorality, and she did not repent. Indeed I will cast her into a sickbed, and those who commit adultery with her into great tribulation, unless they repent of their deeds. I will kill her children with death, and all the churches

shall know that I am he who searches the minds and
hearts. And I will give to each one of you according to
your works.

— Revelation 2:21–23

These are very strong words. When Jesus says, 'I will kill
her children,' he is referring to those who have followed her
teachings. Those who manifest the fruit of her teachings in
their lifestyles are, in essence, her children. Jesus' promise of
judgement on those in the church of Thyatira for tolerating
Jezebel and not repenting was his most severe judgement on
any of the seven churches. I believe this communicates the
intensity of his passion in purging the Church of this spirit.

I see the baby in Rebecca's dream as a picture of the new
prophetic song that the Church is supposed to nurture and
release. But Jezebel is out to kill the prophets (remember
Elijah's story). Her song of death (the mermaid or siren song)
is destroying the prophetic movement; either by overtly per-
secuting and killing the prophets, like she did in the days of
Ahab, or by covertly seducing them into sin, as Balaam and
Balak did with the nation of Israel. By choosing to continue
in their lifestyles of sin, unrepentant, the Israelites were basically inviting the judgement of God on themselves. The baby
being sick to the point of death in Rebecca's dream gives us a
picture of what happens when the spirit of Jezebel is tolerated
in the Church. As Jesus says in Revelation 2, a tolerance of
the activities of Jezebel and an absence of true repentance will
eventually lead to the judgement of God.

A significant shift came in the dream when Rebecca and the mother started to repent of the mermaid spirit. This is exactly what Jesus wanted the church of Thyatira to do – both those who were tolerating Jezebel and those directly involved with her: repent. As Rebecca and the mother repented of this spirit of Jezebel, the baby got better. Repentance will bring a restoration of life, a consecration to our sound, leading to a release and strengthening of the true prophetic move of God in the Church once again. Just as the baby came to health through repentance, I believe the repentance Rebecca was going through in the dream was also representative of the shift that came in her life when the Lord challenged her on the music she had been listening to.

In the next part of the dream Rebecca became Lou Engle, who is known as a Nazirite, an intercessor, a prophet, one raised up to throw Jezebel down. This part of the dream speaks of a special grace that God wants to release over the prophetic worship movement to throw Jezebel down and reclaim the position of influence that she has occupied over a generation. The pathway to walking in this authority is repentance, consecration and intercession.

The £1 coin represents the riches and exploits that the enemy has stolen, but also spiritual authority. In the United Kingdom, our pound coins carry the face of the Queen. She has authority over the nation, and even though she is not a politician she possesses the power to dismiss a Prime Minister (a ruler) from office.

It seems to me that Rebecca finding this coin in her dream is symbolic and prophetic of the consecrated, praying Church regaining the influence that the spirit of Jezebel has enjoyed over the nation. This reminds me of what Jesus promises the church of Thyatira if they overcome Jezebel's influence: in Revelation 2:26, he says, 'And he who overcomes, and keeps my works until the end, to him I will give power over the nations.' I believe God is calling the Church to dethrone Jezebel and take back what the enemy has stolen from us. Just as in the sexual revolution of the '60s, the Church has handed Jezebel (immorality) its position of authority and influence, but God wants to restore the voice of the Church – a voice that is wholly consecrated to him.

We have let the music of the world seep into church. We have given it our voice and our sound. Can it be that, in our corporate worship, there's another spirit at work that's seducing our emotions? At home, we are even more addicted to the music of this world and when we come to God to worship him, whether at home or in a church service, we often find ourselves bored and disconnected; could it be that our flesh is so full of the sound of this world that our senses are dulled to the things of the Spirit? It's time for repentance and a re-consecration of our sound.

There are certain sounds that can carry an anointing that breaks the hold of darkness. These are sounds from heaven that cause demons to flee, and I believe God wants to release these sounds in and through his people in these last days. The problem is that many of those called to walk in this level of authority are not able to be used by God to release such breakthrough because their sound has been diluted and contaminated by other sounds that they have lent their ears to. Their ears have not been consecrated to his sound, so their voices lack his manifest authority. They may be great musicians or singers but their gift is not carrying the necessary power and authority to destroy the hold of the enemy over a generation.

As we saw in Chapter 1, before John the Baptist could become 'the voice' he first had to become 'the ear.' The reason his voice carried such authority in bringing conviction of sin and deliverance to the masses was the depth of his consecration to God. In the wilderness, John didn't have a medley of sounds and voices competing for his attention. He set himself apart to tune into God's voice, while tuning out all other influences. He placed such a consecration on his ears that when he was eventually given the opportunity to voice the thing that he had been set apart to tune into for so many years, his voice shook the very fabric of a nation.

THE POWER OF AGREEMENT

Agreement is such a powerful weapon in advancing God's purposes in our lives, but just like a sword in the wrong hands, it can do the same job for the agenda of the enemy. Coming into agreement with God releases his power in our lives.

In Genesis 11, we read of an incident that illustrates the power of agreement. At the time, the whole earth was of one language and the people decided to build a tower that would reach to 'the heavens'. Ultimately, they wanted to make a name for themselves. Here's what God had to say about their agreement:

> The LORD said, 'If as one people speaking the same language they have begun to do this, then nothing they plan to do will be impossible for them.'
>
> — Genesis 11:6

I think it's amazing that God said this! Even though the people had set their hearts on doing something that was against his purposes. God acknowledged that nothing would be impossible for them because of the agreement they had together in speaking the same language and setting their hearts on the same objective. The only way God could stop them was to confuse their language, which obviously resulted in a lack of agreement.

In Acts 2, on the day of Pentecost, we see another amazing picture of the power of agreement. The disciples had been praying together for several days, waiting in the upper room for the promise of the Holy Spirit. On the tenth day of being together, we read this:

> When the Day of Pentecost had fully come, they were
> all with one accord in one place.
>
> — Acts 2:1

Here we see that the disciples were not just physically together, they were in one accord, which speaks of agreement at a heart level. As a secondary consequence of their obedience to the Lord in waiting for the baptism of the Holy Spirit, and their agreement with each other by being in one accord, there was a release of what the Lord had promised. Agreement is a powerful weapon, both for good and for evil.

Having looked briefly at the power of agreement between individuals, we should also consider another level of agreement that we don't often think about: the agreement within ourselves. Let's look at the agreement between the 'ear gate' and the 'mouth gate'.

EARS AND MOUTH

As a child, I really didn't like taking pills when I was ill. Actually, I don't think I've changed much as an adult! I still remember the horrible taste, and they sometimes got stuck in my throat when I struggled to swallow them. My mum would have to try and hide them in my food to make it easier for me. I've heard of other people crushing the tablets and mixing them with something sweet to try and mask the bitter taste when their child has to take a pill. As Mary Poppins says: 'A spoonful of sugar helps the medicine go down.'

In many ways, the pill is like those poisonous, negative and ungodly words that the enemy wants to inject into our lives, and I believe music can often play the role of the sugar that helps the medicine go down. Once something has made its way into our hearts through our ear gate, our mouth and voice eventually start to align with it.

Over the years, I have heard believers singing along to songs with words that they would never usually speak in conversation. Somehow, the music seems to give the ungodly message a way in. I believe this is a strategy of the enemy to get into our hearts and neutralise our authority. The ears receive the seed of deception through sugar-coated music, and – left unchallenged – this seed leads to conception in the heart.

Finally and inevitably, the mouth gives birth to that which was conceived in the heart. The enemy's goal is not just to get a lie into your heart through your ear gate but to birth it through your mouth gate, and we must guard against this. Addressing the Pharisees in Matthew 12:34, Jesus says, 'Out of the abundance of the heart the mouth speaks,' meaning that the words we speak are an overflow of whatever is already stored up in our hearts.

Once the mouth of a believer begins to speak or sing that which originated in the kingdom of darkness, they are basically coming into agreement with the enemy, and thereby giving him authority in that area of their lives. As a believer, you cannot surrender your vocal chords to ungodly and depraved ideologies all week long and then somehow expect a move of God on Sunday, when you sing 'Spirit break out...'. There is a mixture, a corruption, in your sound which makes you lack the authority necessary to release the true sound of heaven. I believe the Lord will pour out his Spirit without measure if he finds a people without mixture.

Music that is born of the flesh and influenced by the kingdom of darkness has certain traits, and if we took the time to fully examine them we would be in no doubt that a true child of God has no business letting these things into their lives. I am not saying that every song we listen to has to have 'Jesus, I love you' in the lyrics, but my point is that many of the songs that are popular and prominent in our culture today clearly glorify the flesh, immorality and things that are fundamentally opposed to the nature of the Holy Spirit. Why should we be friendly with a system and a culture that is opposed to everything Christ died for?

> Do you not know that friendship with the world is enmity with God? Whoever therefore wants to be a friend of the world makes himself an enemy of God.
>
> — James 4:4

'The world' in this verse refers to a demonic system that is set up to propagate the agenda of the devil. Obviously, this is different to 'the world' that Jesus refers to in John 3:16: 'For God so loved the world that he gave his only begotten son that whosoever believes in him must not die but have eternal life.' God loves the people of the world but hates the sinful culture of the world.

EYES AND EARS

The eye gate and the ear gate are key points of influence for the spirit of Jezebel. In fact, I would go as far as saying that it is mainly through one or both of these senses that the spirit of Jezebel influences the lives of individuals. These are the two primary gateways into the heart and soul of a person.

Let's look at an interesting passage in 1 Samuel. Saul, the king of Israel, is under some sort of oppression and only David's playing of the harp brings him any relief.

> And so it was, whenever the spirit from God was upon Saul, that David would take a harp and play it with his hand. Then Saul would become refreshed and well, and the distressing spirit would depart from him.
>
> — 1 Samuel 16:23

When the writer of the book of Samuel talks of an evil or distressing spirit 'from God', some may find this confusing as God is not the author of evil. I think a helpful way to understand this verse is that it was 'an evil spirit that God permitted'. The evil spirit that came on Saul was not from God in the sense that God was afflicting or tempting Saul with evil. Saul had opened himself up to demonic oppression through his disobedience to God. God, however, permitted the evil spirit to oppress Saul. When David played the harp, the distressing spirit would depart from Saul: here we have a picture of deliverance through anointed music.

Music carries a presence, and presence changes atmospheres. Certain behavioural patterns are more prevalent in certain atmospheres; for example, in the environment of a night club you're likely to find drunkenness and promiscuity. I believe this has a lot to do with the atmosphere that has been nurtured in such places, and music plays a major role in nurturing an atmosphere. The type of presence carried by certain music is discernible from the fruit produced in the lives of the hearers of that music. When David played the harp and the sound entered Saul's ears, the demons fled. Saul's ear gate was the pathway to his deliverance.

Music gets into the soul through the ears. If Saul got delivered simply by listening to music that was anointed by the Holy Spirit then could it be possible to get oppressed through demonically 'anointed' music? If the demons were played out then could they also be played in? I have often wondered about this.

There is a whole lot of demonically inspired music today – more than ever, I think. It is not uncommon for people to listen to certain music and feel weighed down with depression, even being compelled to self-harm. While, on the one hand, Holy Spirit inspired music will influence its listeners with godly desires (peace, hope, joy), demonically inspired music will often influence its listeners with a strong desire for immorality. Other times, people will listen to music inspired by the devil (without realising it) and will get filled with rage and a spirit of violence. The enemy is using the ear gate as a major pathway to influence souls *en masse*. Remember: the spirit of Jezebel is a spirit of seduction. Music is one of the avenues through which this spirit influences the lives of many.

GUARDING YOUR HEART

I do love travelling, but I am less of a fan of going through security at the airport. If you haven't been abroad recently, allow me to update you. The current limit on how much liquid or gel you can carry onto a plane in a single container is 100ml. If you need to take more than one 100ml container, all of your 100ml containers must be carried in a clear plastic bag, and it must be easy to open and close. Oh, and you can only take one of these bags on board. On more than one occasion, I've got to airport security and suddenly realised that I've left my aftershave or lotion in my rucksack, meaning I have no choice but to throw it away at the checkpoint. And that stuff's not cheap!

The security staff at airports are just doing their job, and their job is to get rid of anything that might turn out to be harmful to passengers or crew. They have to be ruthless and can't concern themselves with how annoyed you might feel about having to chuck out that aftershave, because their top priority is the safety of every person on the flight. A lot of these strict security measures came into place after the 9/11 terror attack on the USA, when four planes were hijacked and almost 3,000 people lost their lives. Since then, the statistics show that plane hijackings have dramatically decreased. In the year 2000, there were about 26 hijacking incidents. After 9/11, there were 10 in 2002, nine in 2003, four in 2004, and only one in 2005. That's a 96% decline in five years. It seems highly likely that this dramatic decrease is at least partly due to the heightened security checks and stricter rules on what you can take onto a commercial flight.

The kingdom of darkness is in the business of hijacking people's minds. So many minds have been hijacked and are heading for destruction, all because of poor security checks at the eye gate and the ear gate. If you don't want your mind hijacked by the enemy, you have to apply strict security checks at these vital entry points.

As we've seen, the eye and ear gates are the two main pathways into the heart and soul of an individual. I believe Solomon knew this and that's why he admonishes us to guard our hearts:

> Keep and guard your heart with all vigilance and above
> all that you guard, for out of it flow the springs of life.
> — Proverbs 4:23 (AMP)

The first part of this verse encourages us to guard the inroads to our hearts, while the second part emphasises that whatever gets into our hearts eventually finds its way into our lives.

Guarding your heart involves keeping a strict, vigilant and close watch on what you're letting in. What goes in eventually affects what comes out. To guard the heart is to put a safeguard, a security system, on what we listen to (ear gate) and what we watch (eye gate).

It's more challenging to get the enemy off the flight once he's already on board and the plane is airborne. You cannot be lenient with the enemy at your gates and then wonder why you're constantly struggling with lust, bitterness, depression, or whatever it may be. You cannot have a low standard at your gates and not expect hijackings in the air.

In warfare, whichever side has air supremacy will enjoy a significant advantage. According to Ephesians 2:2, the enemy is known as 'the prince of the power of the air, the spirit who now works in the sons of disobedience.' The enemy's influence 'in the air' is manifested in the lifestyles of the individuals who let him in through their gates. In the life of an unbeliever, there are no security checks, and the enemy can wander through the gates unchallenged – he has free reign. The only way to stop him is by first surrendering one's life to the Lordship of Jesus Christ.

In the life of a believer, the enemy is desperate to gain influence by accessing our gates (and thereby influencing our lifestyles). His weapons of destruction are filtering through the gateways of so many Christians today, unchallenged. The result is that the enemy gains air supremacy in our lives, and we are neutralised in our authority and unable to effect real change for the kingdom of God.

Even with the strictest of security checks and procedures, there are still times when illegal items manage to slip through the gates. Martin Luther once said, 'You cannot keep birds from flying over your head but you can keep them from building a nest in your hair.' Our world is filled with so much pollution, perversion and darkness that the eye and ear gates are often bombarded with dangerous images, words and ideologies – it's almost unavoidable. But we must be alert and intentional about allowing the water of the word to cleanse our souls of these things on a regular basis.

> You are already *clean because of the word* which I have spoken to you.
>   — John 15:3 (emphasis added)

> Husbands, love your wives, just as Christ also loved the church and gave himself for her, that he might sanctify and *cleanse her with the washing of water by the word*, that he might present her to himself a glorious church, not having spot or wrinkle or any such thing, but that she should be holy and without blemish.
>   — Ephesians 5:25–27 (emphasis added)

We need to live with such an awareness of our thought life that we refuse to entertain thoughts in our hearts, about ourselves or about others, that do not exist in God's heart. If we don't take our thoughts captive, they will eventually take us captive. There is a massive difference between a rigorous security system that occasionally fails and lets an illegal item slip through, and a weak to non-existent security check that will allow just about anything in. The former is active while the latter is passive. We are supposed to have an active security system at the eye and ear gates.

POSSESS THE ENEMY'S GATE

The Lord gave Abraham a promise that his descendants would possess the gate of their enemies. This was not just a promise to the Israelites in a physical sense, but one that also applies to the New Testament believer in a spiritual sense, as the apostle Paul teaches in Galatians.

> '...blessing I will bless you, and multiplying I will multiply your descendants as the stars of the heaven and as the sand which is on the seashore; and your descendants *shall possess the gate of their enemies.*'
>
> — Genesis 22:17-19 (emphasis added)

> And if you are Christ's, then you are Abraham's seed, and heirs according to the promise.
>
> — Galatians 3:29

When Jesus said, 'I will build my Church and the gates of hell will not prevail,' he did not mean that the Church would be on the defensive. On the contrary, the gates of hell will not prevail because the Church is on the offensive. We are called to possess the gate of the enemy, but we cannot possess the gate of the enemy if he has already possessed our gates. It's time to kick the enemy off the flight and regain air supremacy in our lives. How? By allowing the Holy Spirit to repossess our gates so that we can be effective in possessing the gates of the enemy.

To guard the heart is to improve the security system at the eye and ear gates, being extremely careful and strict about what is allowed in. This is important because the heart is like an incubator: when certain words, images or thoughts get into the heart unchallenged, they fester for a while. They are kept hidden and allowed to grow and mature, waiting patiently for a day of manifestation. Often, we don't even know what's in our heart. But when it has been incubated and quietly nurtured for some time, it matures and eventually manifests itself as a strong emotion, or a pattern of thought or behaviour.

Once something ungodly gets in via the eye or ear gate, we must be conscious and intentional about getting it out via the word of God, repentance, and the blood of Jesus; otherwise, it is like an infection that will eventually begin to control our emotions, decisions and lifestyle. This is why we need to guard what goes in because, in the long run, what goes in ends up shaping how we live. Unless it is uprooted and destroyed, it will eventually and inevitably manifest in some way in our lives.

How is your security system at your eye and ear gate? Has the enemy hijacked your mind because of poor security checks? It's not too late to kick the enemy off the flight. Join me in this simple prayer:

Heavenly Father, I confess that I have allowed the enemy easy access to my heart by not being vigilant about what I have allowed in through my eye gate and my ear gate. Lord, I'm sorry for this. Forgive me for my sinful actions. I rededicate my eyes, my ears and my mouth to you. Every seed of perversion, deception and pollution planted in my heart by the enemy, I command to be completely uprooted and destroyed in Jesus' name. I break off the influence of the enemy over my eyes, ears and mouth. Holy Spirit, help me to have a higher level of security at my gates. Help me to be vigilant, sensitive, discerning and not ignorant of the devices of the enemy. In Jesus' name I pray. Amen!

CHAPTER SIX

BRING THE FIRE

The power of sacrifice and consecration

Rebecca once shared with me a strange experience that had stuck with her from her teenage years. One afternoon, she went out to do some shopping in Manchester city centre. When she was finished, she sat on a bench and was watching the water fountains at Piccadilly Gardens, when a young man in his early 20s walked past her with his friend. Even before it happened, she somehow knew that he was going to approach her. At first, he glanced around and then walked away as if he hadn't noticed her, but a few minutes later he came back. This time, he walked straight up to Rebecca and asked if she would like a KitKat. She politely declined but he kept insisting until she took it. Even stranger than this pushy behaviour, as she looked into his eyes to say no, his pupils changed colour to a glowing red! She was so shocked and afraid that she took the KitKat from him and got on the bus to go home, feeling sure that something was going on with this guy and wondering what on earth to do with this little chocolate bar. However, she felt compelled to not just throw it away or give it to someone else. While still on the bus, she decided to drop it on the floor in a corner and trample on it until it was unrecognisable and in pieces.

When Rebecca told me all this, I felt like this guy was an agent of the enemy and on a mission to draw certain people into witchcraft. I know that may seem like an overly dramatic assessment of a slightly odd encounter in the street, but you need to understand that I grew up in Nigeria, in a culture where things like this were very common.

I moved to the UK when I was 17, and until that point, I had never met an atheist my whole life. It's not that everyone I met while I lived in Nigeria was a Christian, it's just that people in that culture are very aware of the spiritual world so even if they don't believe in Jesus, they believe in something spiritual. Sometimes, people in the West think of witchcraft as something that's not real or that only exists in parts of Africa and certain 'less developed' nations. Having lived in the UK for over 19 years, I can tell you from experience that witchcraft is very real over here too. Like so many things, it's just been repackaged for the western mind.

So when Rebecca shared her experience with me, I sensed that this was some form of initiation. That particular KitKat was not just an innocent chocolate bar, it was food that had been sacrificed to demonic idols, and I believe that if Rebecca had eaten it she would have been coming into fellowship with the spirit behind that gift. At this point, she wasn't living a fully surrendered life to Jesus. The enemy already had inroads in her life through her ear gate and her eye gate, and now he wanted to get in through her mouth gate, with demonic food for the purpose of initiation.

Back in Chapter 4, we looked at Jesus' words to the church of Thyatira. In his correction to them, Jesus made reference to them being taught and seduced to eat things sacrificed to idols:

> Nevertheless I have a few things against you, because you allow that woman Jezebel, who calls herself a prophetess, to teach and seduce my servants to commit sexual immorality and eat things sacrificed to idols.
>
> — Revelation 2:20

Notice that Jezebel's strategy here, as described by Jesus, involves not just sexual immorality but also eating. And Jesus didn't specifically say 'food' sacrificed to idols but rather 'things' sacrificed to idols. What she was seducing people to eat was not just ordinary food as we know it, but sacrifices, and these sacrifices were things that the Lord did not consider food. Strong's Bible Concordance identifies the original Greek for the phrase 'things sacrificed to idols' as *eidōlothytos*, which literally means the flesh left over from heathen sacrifices. Jezebel was pretty much seducing the church to partake in demonic rituals. Jezebel's table is the place where these 'things' (flesh) are served.

In Chapter 2, we took a brief look at the sin of Peor, where Balaam advised Balak to use the Moabite women to seduce Israelite men into attending their fertility festival, involving Baal worship and sexual immorality. We find this account in Numbers 25:

> Now Israel remained in Acacia Grove, and the people began to commit harlotry with the women of Moab. They invited the people to the sacrifices of their gods, and the people ate and bowed down to their gods. So Israel was joined to Baal of Peor, and the anger of the Lord was aroused against Israel.
>
> — Numbers 25:1–3

Isn't it interesting that the way in which the children of Israel were seduced by sexual immorality and eating sacrifices is the exact same way the church of Thyatira and (as we will see later in this chapter) the wider Church today is being seduced to eat sacrifices? I am convinced it is the same spirit at work. To understand a bit more about the significance of eating things sacrificed to idols, let's dive deeper into the concept of sacrifice.

ANIMAL SACRIFICE

We know from the Old Testament that animal sacrifice by priests was the main method for atoning for sins under the old covenant. All these sacrifices pointed to the ultimate sacrifice, which was Jesus' own blood shed to atone for the sins of humanity.

Jesus' sacrifice on the cross nullified the need for the ongoing atonement of sin through the sacrifice of animals. Many Gentiles (non-Jews), turning to Christ in the early Church, would have come from a background of pagan worship, where animal sacrifice was a part of their lifestyle. For the Jews, though, the difference was that the sacrifices we see prescribed in the Torah (the five books of Moses) were all instigated by God and had to be performed in a specific manner, because they all in fact pointed to Jesus. Pagan sacrifices were not carried out with this prophetic symbolism in mind but were inspired by demons. In his letter to the Corinthians, Paul makes it very clear that the sacrifices performed to idols by Gentiles were, in reality, sacrifices to demons.

> Rather, that the things which the Gentiles sacrifice they *sacrifice to demons* and not to God, and I do not want you to have *fellowship* with demons.
> — 1 Corinthians 10:20 (emphasis added)

This also tells us that sacrifice is a means of fellowship. So, in actual fact, these sacrifices offered by pagans were one of the ways in which the people fellowshipped with demons, whether knowingly or unknowingly.

Throughout scripture, it is very clear that sacrifice is a major part of worship. Just as this is true with Jehovah God, the same is also true in the kingdom of darkness. In fact, when you think about it, animal sacrifice plays a key role in many of the world's religions. Why is sacrifice so important, both in the kingdom of God and in the kingdom of darkness? I think the answer to that is one word: blood.

THE MYSTERY OF BLOOD SACRIFICE

Blood, in essence, is the very life of a living thing. Many don't appreciate the power in blood. I have come to realise that blood has different dimensions of power: for example, the blood of a chicken, the blood of a spotless lamb, the blood of an unborn baby in the womb, the blood of a newborn baby, the blood of a virgin woman, and the blood of a fully grown adult man all have varying degrees of potency in the realm of the spirit. Blood is one of the major currencies of transaction in this realm. The shedding of blood in sacrifice releases power in the realm of the spirit, which can be used either positively to advance the kingdom of God (as we will see shortly) or negatively to advance the agenda of darkness. Having heard many testimonies of individuals who were involved in the occult before having a radical encounter with Jesus and surrendering their lives to him, I have come to realise that those with first hand experience of the occult and witchcraft often seem to understand the power of a blood sacrifice and its impact in the spirit realm a whole lot more than many believers. Let's take a look at a classic incident in the Bible that gives us an insight into this mystery.

In 2 Kings 3 we read a very interesting account, where Jehoram (king of Israel) joins forces with Jehoshaphat (king of Judah), and the king of Edom, to fight against the king of Moab. They call for Elisha to prophecy about the impending battle, and Elisha shows up and prophecies victory for the three kings. The word of the Lord to them is that he (the Lord) will also deliver the Moabites into their hands:

> And this is a simple matter in the sight of the Lord;
> he will also deliver the Moabites into your hand. Also
> you shall attack every fortified city and every choice
> city, and shall cut down every good tree, and stop up
> every spring of water, and ruin every good piece of
> land with stones.
>
> — 2 Kings 3:18–19

It's worth noting the spiritual stature of the guy who prophesied this. I mean, this is Elisha: the double portion prophet who had a strong track record of being accurate in his prophetic ministry. However, something very unusual happened on the battlefield:

And when the king of Moab saw that the battle was too fierce for him, he took with him seven hundred men who drew swords, to break through to the king of Edom, but they could not. Then *he took his eldest son who would have reigned in his place, and offered him as a burnt offering upon the wall*; and there was great indignation against Israel. So they departed from him and returned to their own land.

— 2 Kings 3:26–27 (emphasis added)

Even though Elisha released a prophetic word about victory, that's not what appears to have happened. How was that possible? Sacrifice! And not just any sacrifice, either: a high price blood sacrifice. As you can see from the passage above, when the king of Moab saw that he was losing the battle and that there was no way out for him, he deployed his deadliest weapon: the sacrifice of his eldest son. The magnitude of the sacrifice released something so significant in the realm of the spirit, empowering demonic forces in such a way that the resulting manifestation in the natural realm was great indignation against Israel. The quality of the blood that was shed (i.e. his eldest son) released the magnitude of power that turned the battle against Israel. Even though they had the prophetic word from the Lord that they were going to win, that prophetic word did not become a reality because the enemy out-sacrificed the people of God.

The point I'm trying to make is not that the people of God need to enter into human sacrifice in order to overcome the enemy, but I want to focus your attention on the power of the blood sacrifice in the realm of the spirit. What Israel experienced on this battlefield that led to them returning home after facing great indignation was not of natural causes but of supernatural influence, invoked by the mystery of the blood sacrifice. This is precisely why the blood of Jesus is so powerful. One of the major weapons we have against the enemy in spiritual warfare is the blood of Jesus. The only begotten son of God (the highest possible price) was sacrificed on the cross for the sins of the world.

The miraculous circumstances surrounding Jesus' conception help to signal to us that his blood was divine. This is why, when his blood was shed, it carried such incomprehensible ranking and value in the spirit realm. It was literally like Jesus' blood caused the enemy complete bankruptcy, never to recover again. There is no other blood currency in heaven, on earth or under the earth that could come close to the potency of what is made available in the blood of Jesus. The blood that was shed on Calvary was not any ordinary blood; it was God's blood! There is such power in the blood of Jesus: the enemy knows this and he absolutely hates it. There is more power in one drop of the blood of Jesus than in all of the kingdom of darkness and demons of hell combined. Hallelujah!

THE LORD'S TABLE

Jesus said a lot of very unusual things that were unintelligible to his listeners, without the help of the Holy Spirit. Very few of those listening to him really understood the depth of a lot of what he taught. Here's an example, from the book of John, where Jesus says something that completely takes everyone by surprise and even drives a lot of his followers away. Even his disciples didn't know what to make of this:

> Those who *eat my flesh* and *drink my blood* have eternal life, and I will raise them up on the last day. My flesh is true food, and my blood is true drink. Those who eat my flesh and drink my blood live in me, and I live in them.
>
> — John 6:54–56 (emphasis added)

His audience were Jewish, so the mere mention of this was offensive in their culture. I do not think Jesus expected the people listening to him to literally eat his flesh and drink his blood, but the reality of this declaration is made manifest when we partake of the Lord's table in Holy Communion together. During the Last Supper, Jesus' actions shed more light on what he meant in John 6:

> And he took bread, gave thanks and broke it, and gave it to them, saying, 'This is *my body* which is given for you; do this in remembrance of me.' Likewise he also

> took the cup after supper, saying, 'This cup is the new
> covenant in *my blood*, which is shed for you.'
> — Luke 22:19–20 (emphasis added)

We are only able to partake of the body and the blood of Jesus in communion because of his sacrifice. The highest price was paid. When we partake at the Lord's table, as we eat the bread (his body) and drink the grape juice (his blood), we are coming into union with Christ himself.

Offering sacrifices was one of the important functions of a priest under the old covenant. The Lord told Moses to command the priests to not just offer the sacrifices but also to eat them (Leviticus 6:25-26). Why? I believe this was because the sacrifices, and the manner in which the priests partook of them, were a foreshadow of the New Testament act of communion, which Jesus instituted just before he went to the cross, offering himself as the spotless Lamb of God who was sacrificed for the sins of the world.

As believers under the new covenant, when we come to the Lord's table we are priests (1 Peter 2:9), partaking of the sacrifice of the Lamb of God – the body and the blood of Jesus. In doing so, we enter into fellowship and a common union with the Lord. Similarly, those sacrificing to idols would often partake of the sacrifice, and this was a form of satanic communion – anyone partaking of this sacrifice also came into fellowship with the demons. Paul alludes to this when he says, 'the things which the Gentiles sacrifice they sacrifice to demons and not to God, and I do not want you to have fellowship with demons.' We know that the enemy does not have the power to create but only to copy, pervert and counterfeit God's original design. Deep occult and witchcraft practices often involve drinking blood, eating flesh and offering sacrifices. They do this as a way of increasing in union with demon spirits and satanic powers. This is an act of spiritual warfare by the kingdom of darkness against the people of God. However, in the book of Revelation, John writes about one of our most powerful weapons against the enemy:

> And they overcame him by *the blood* of the Lamb and by *the word* of their testimony, and they *did not love their lives to the death*.
>
> — Revelation 12:11 (emphasis added)

The saints overcame the enemy in spiritual warfare by three things: the blood, the word and lives laid down. This is one of the reasons why communion is such a powerful form of spiritual warfare. The blood referenced here is a picture of the wine or juice we take during communion, while 'the word' is a picture of bread, the body of Jesus. 'They did not love their lives to death' speaks of our complete surrender to the Lord, which is critical for being effective in spiritual warfare (James 4:7).

EATING SPIRITUALLY-CONTAMINATED FOOD

Sometimes food is one of the ways in which the powers of witchcraft are used to attack people. I experienced this myself some years ago, when I was invited to speak at a church. At the end of the service I was at the back of the church, greeting and speaking to people, when a young lady who I had never met before approached me. As we talked, she made reference to how she and her mother had only recently started coming to this church and had joined the food committee. Sure enough, after the service, some refreshments were being laid out so she went over to where the food was being served and got me some of the snacks that she and her mother had helped to prepare. I did feel a check in my spirit but as the day went on I forgot about this unease and ended up eating the snack.

Later, on our way home, my wife said she had felt something strange about this woman. Rebecca hadn't been standing with me at the time, but was close by when the lady approached me and brought me the snack. I admitted that I had felt a check in my spirit about it too, but by this point I had eaten the food and noticed something strange happening to me. It seemed as though my thoughts were unusually obsessed with this lady. It was like I couldn't get her off my mind, in a very strange way. Along with the thoughts came also a strong desire to search for her online. Thankfully, I'm usually open with my wife about everything. So the moment I noticed what was going on, I told Rebecca, and we knew that what I was feeling was connected to the food I had eaten. I wasn't sensitive to the Holy Spirit and so I repented to the Lord and started to take a stand against this pollution in my desires. I started to pray, 'Lord, cleanse me from every inward toleration of the spirit of Jezebel.' A few days passed before I felt the influence of this spirit completely broken off me. But I learnt a valuable lesson through this experience.

It is important to be aware that food can be one of the strategies for Jezebel to influence people's lives. It is crucial that we are sensitive to the Holy Spirit and always bless food before eating. If we are disobedient to the leading of the Holy Spirit and eat what we shouldn't eat, then blessing the food will not nullify the spiritual contamination in the food. There are ministers of the gospel who have come under the control of the spirit of Jezebel because of items, particularly food, that were received from individuals hosting this spirit, with an agenda from the kingdom of darkness.

Think about it: why was eating a major strategy for Jezebel in seducing the church of Thyatira? Remember, Adam and Eve fell to the seduction of the enemy in the garden of Eden through the temptation of eating something that they knew they shouldn't eat; Jesus' first temptation after a 40-day fast centred on turning stone to bread so that he could eat; and in the book of Revelation, the spirit of Jezebel is seducing the church of Thyatira to eat. Jezebel's strategy here is connected to the stirring up of ungodly appetites: in Adam's case it was appetite for forbidden knowledge; in Jesus' case the temptation was an attempt to play into the appetite for personal gain through dysfunction of identity; and with the church of Thyatira it was appetite for satisfaction through selfish fleshly desires, which ultimately led to communion with demons. In essence, by eating food sacrificed to idols the church became partakers of satanic altars and partakers of the table of demons (a perversion and counterfeit of the Lord's table). This was a way of bringing them into fellowship and communion with demon spirits, and thereby neutralising their authority. The pathway the enemy took to arrive at this destination was their appetite.

JEZEBEL'S TABLE

Through Elijah's declaration to King Ahab (1 Kings 17), the heavens were shut over the nation and there was a drought in the land for three and a half years. When the Lord was about to send rain, he spoke to Elijah to present himself to Ahab again. This time around, Elijah told Ahab to gather all the prophets of Baal and Asherah for a bout on Mount Carmel.

> Now therefore, send and gather all Israel to me on Mount Carmel, the four hundred and fifty prophets of Baal, and the four hundred prophets of Asherah, *who eat at Jezebel's table.*
>
> — 1 Kings 18:19 (emphasis added)

Earlier in this chapter, we discussed the Lord's table and how communion is a form of spiritual warfare. Well, Jezebel's table was also a table of communion, albeit a perverted counterfeit of the original!

Remember, in Revelation 2:20, Jesus said that Jezebel seduced the Thyatira church to commit sexual immorality and to eat 'things sacrificed to idols'. Again, the Greek word here is *eidōlothytos*, which means: the flesh left over from heathen sacrifices. So, what kind of flesh was this? Animal flesh? Human flesh? We don't know for sure. However, as I have said, I believe sacrifices carry varying degrees of weight in the realm of the spirit. The king of Edom did not sacrifice an animal to turn the battle against Israel in 2 Kings 3, he sacrificed his eldest son. Why? Because there was such a high value in the realm of the spirit for his son's blood and flesh. Notice that it wasn't just his son, it was his eldest son, who was in line to the throne.

In the spirit realm, the highest bidder often tends to be the one with the upper hand in a given situation. The church of Thyatira may not have been eating human flesh but I wouldn't be surprised if Jezebel herself did eat human flesh. Jezebel's table in 1 Kings 18:19 would most likely have had flesh sacrificed on it. The prophets of Baal and Asherah most likely would have engaged in the ritual of eating human flesh and drinking blood. The eating of human flesh is a common practice in high level witchcraft, and we know Jezebel was involved in a lot of witchcraft. Jehu made that clear when he was on his way to destroy her.

Now it happened, when Joram saw Jehu, that he said,
'Is it peace, Jehu?' So he answered, 'What peace, as
long as the harlotries of your mother Jezebel and her
witchcraft are so many?'

— 2 Kings 9:22

I understand that what I am about to share next may be
alarming and completely foreign to some. I don't want to shy
away from the fact that the kingdom of darkness is very real
and these things do happen today. But we don't need to be
scared of the enemy when we are living in the light and in
submission to God's authority.

Some years ago I came across the testimony of an ex-Satanist, James Kawalya, from Uganda. James became a witchdoctor at the age of three, and by the age of seven was so
deeply immersed in the occult that he became a territorial
ruler over southern Uganda and northern Tanzania. As he
grew in his influence in the kingdom of darkness, he was
often sent on assignments to kill people, destroy churches etc.
He was once sent to destroy a small church of 20 women
and one man – the pastor. The prayers from this church were
causing much disruption to the works of the enemy in the
spirit realm. This was because the members of the church had
made a covenant with one another to pray for six consecutive
hours, every day for 90 days. Before they started this prayer
marathon they decided that if any of them came late to the
prayer meeting, or couldn't attend for whatever reason, they

would all have to start again from day one. So, the prayer marathon started with agreement.

The prayers from this church were shifting the spiritual atmosphere of their region and nation. They even started causing significant breakthroughs for the kingdom of God in other nations. With all this going on, it's not surprising that they became a key target for the enemy. Many witches were sent to destroy the church but failed. However, James Kawalya was successful in his assignment. Afterwards, he was summoned to travel to Rome to meet the leaders of a secret society called the black Jesuits, where he thought he was going to be honoured and rewarded for the great work he had accomplished in destroying this church. It was on his way to this meeting that James had a powerful encounter with Jesus and was radically saved. He later discovered, through one of the members of the society who had since become a Christian, that their plan had been to sacrifice his body and eat his flesh because they believed he now carried a higher level of energy and power. Over the years, I've got to know James Kawalya personally, and he is an anointed man of God. The Lord uses him greatly in exposing the works of darkness and bringing deliverance to people under the yoke of demonic oppression.

The eating of flesh and the drinking of blood all seems gross and disgusting to many of us today, but let's not think we are immune to partaking of Jezebel's table. Remember that the 'things sacrificed to idols' refers to the church of Thyatira being seduced to eat the leftover flesh from heathen sacrifices. So, in essence, Jezebel's table is where flesh is freely put on display for consumption; works of the flesh on display to satisfy the appetites of the sinful nature.

I would say that this sums up what a lot of today's media is all about – 'flesh on display for consumption' – but what's even more shocking and sad is that the same thing is also going on within many churches. It might be sugar-coated with 'spirituality' but what we have in reality is works of the flesh on display. In these end times, there is far too much flesh marketing going on in many of our pulpits: weapons of mass distraction being unleashed from our platforms and carnality being sugar-coated with fake and shallow spirituality.

IDOLATRY

According to Webster's Dictionary, idolatry is the worship of idols or the excessive devotion to or reverence for some person or thing. This is a theme that's strong throughout scriptures, in both the Old and New Testaments. In fact, the first of the Ten Commandments directly prohibits the practice of idolatry.

> You shall have no other gods before me.
>   — Exodus 20:3

Throughout the Old Testament, the children of Israel appear to have had a fascination with idols. It's hard for us, today, to understand why they were seemingly so easily tempted to bow down to a block of wood or stone, but we so often fall into the same temptation. It may look different, we may not be physically bowing down to a statue or a carving, but our lives are often dominated by the worship of idols such as money, materialism, relationships, entertainment, or whatever it may be. An idol is anything that is in an exalted position in our lives, taking the place of God. So idolatry extends beyond physical objects to heart issues.

ENTERTAINMENT-DRIVEN CULTURE

From my own observation, I think one of the strongest appetites of our generation is the need to be entertained. Entertainment seems to be to the soul what food is to the body. And I have come to believe that Jezebel is the main spirit at work in a lot of modern entertainment. This wicked spirit has taken advantage of the appetites of many. Now, through media platforms across the world, a whole genera-tion is being fed the doctrines of demons – in other words, eating at Jezebel's table.

The prophets of Baal and Asherah were promoting sexual immorality all throughout culture, and I think we see this today through the media of film, TV and music. Your TV screens, phones, tablets and computers are like tables upon which the food sacrificed to idols is being served. Eating food sacrificed to idols is partaking at the table of Jezebel; it is communion and fellowship with demons. It's amazing to me how many believers are not sensitive to the Holy Spirit and would watch just about any movie or listen to any music, and think they are immune to its influence because they are under grace. I wonder whether the Holy Spirit would sit comfortably alongside us, in our living rooms or bedrooms, and watch many of the movies, TV shows, or music videos we choose to consume through our screens. I doubt it. It's time to stop tolerating the spirit of Jezebel that has been unleashed through the media, causing masses of people to come into common union with demonic ideologies.

As far back as I can remember I have always had a love for media and video production. When I watched movies I often found myself admiring and being impressed by creative camera shots, composition and visual effects. Rebecca also enjoys watching movies so we would often go out to the cinema or buy a film online to watch together. We later decided to subscribe to Netflix. At the time of writing, Netflix is the world's largest internet streaming entertainment service, with millions of paid memberships in many countries, producing TV series, documentaries and feature films across a wide variety of genres and languages. Members can watch as much as they want – anytime, anywhere, on any internet-connected screen. Members can play, pause and resume watching, all without commercials or commitments.

Rebecca and I don't watch TV often, but we would sometimes decide to watch a film together and then spend a long time scrolling through Netflix to choose our evening's entertainment. Being very aware of not letting anything into our home through the portal of the TV that would grieve the Holy Spirit, we came to a decision that films rated 12 were mostly okay. However, we quickly realised that this general rule wasn't going to work. There were times we would have to turn off the film and repent to the Lord for letting that content into our home.

Before I go on with this story, I'd like to make one point very clear. I do understand that the dealings of the Lord with an individual can be uniquely designed and specific to that individual's calling and assignment on the earth. There are certain things God may not allow me to do that he will seemingly allow another Christian to 'get away with'. We are not talking about sin here, just certain areas where the Holy Spirit starts to require a greater degree of consecration because of the calling the Lord has on the life of an individual. Often, we fall into error or excesses when the personalised dealings of God in the life of an individual are made into a doctrine for all believers.

There are several metaphors used in scripture to describe our relationship with the Lord, or our faith journey. Here, in Hebrews 12, it is the image of a runner:

> Therefore we also, since we are surrounded by so great
> a cloud of witnesses, let us lay aside every weight, and
> the sin which so easily ensnares us, and let us run with
> endurance the race that is set before us.
>
> — Hebrews 12:1

When running a race such as a marathon, the last thing an athlete wants to carry with them is extra weight. A runner tries to be as light as possible. A little extra weight may not seem like a big deal in the moment, but over a long distance it will eventually begin to affect the performance of the athlete. Sin is definitely a weight that slows us down in our faith journey, so we need to get rid of it. But could there be some other weights that are not necessarily sin but are slowing us down even so? I have found this to be true in my relationship with the Lord.

When you begin to go deeper in your intimacy and fellowship with the Lord, he often starts to reveal to you the weights in your life. What the Holy Spirit reveals to me as a weight in my life may not necessarily be what he reveals to you in yours. Regardless, if we want to run the race that's set before us we have to let the weights go. The weights slow us down in our pursuit of God.

Back to my story about Netflix. Over time, I noticed that the movies and shows that were rated 12 would promote certain themes or include scenes or language that made me uncomfortable. It seemed that films rated PG were often the safest to watch, but even then I would sometimes notice themes that made me uneasy. One day, a few years ago, I felt the Lord leading us to cancel our subscription to Netflix. It seemed to me that some of the shows and movies were specifically designed to de-sensitise us to demonic ideologies, and from what I'd seen of the trailers some of the Netflix original content seemed quite dark. I spoke to Rebecca about it and we both agreed it was right for us to cancel our subscription. This wasn't an easy decision but it was a necessary step to take for the sake of obedience and consecration.

My goal in sharing my journey is not to preach that everyone should cancel their Netflix subscriptions (although it would probably do you good), rather my aim is to make you aware of a very strong Jezebelic agenda at work in the media platforms of today. This agenda is set on de-sensitising and indoctrinating a generation with demonic ideologies by enticing us to eat food sacrificed to idols. Your devices (TVs, phones, computers, etc.) are the table you eat from and the things sacrificed to idols are the content you consume. Jezebel's table is alive and well in our culture today.

ACCULTURATION AND CONSECRATION

Acculturation is defined as the cultural modification of an individual, group, or people by adapting to or borrowing traits from another culture. The early settlers in America provide an example of this. They found themselves fighting with the natives, and they devised a plan to avoid this ongoing conflict. The plan was to encourage the natives to increasingly look and speak like them so that they wouldn't seem so threatening and the fighting would cease. So the early settlers began to trade with the natives, teach them English, give them food, etc. and as they became more accustomed to the new culture, conflicts were minimised.

The way acculturation was used by the United States gov-ernment to transform the native American culture gives us a picture of how this spirit of Jezebel is infiltrating and trans-forming many of us believers. Through the arts and enter-tainment and other major spheres of influence in our society, many of us are, without knowing it, going through a process of acculturation to the customs and ideologies of a worldly system that is anti-Christ in nature.

We cannot be used by God to change the world if our life-styles reflect the very systems, ideologies and lifestyle of the world. We cannot bring deliverance to a world whose prin-ciples operate in our souls. This is where consecration comes in once again. We have to be wholly set apart to God while living in this world. To consecrate ourselves to God we have to separate ourselves from the world. This means that, in our lifestyles, we have to separate ourselves from the demonic, Jezebelic systems and ideologies operating in this world.

It's not just about being 'separated from' the world but rather it's more about being 'separated unto' the Lord. Consecration is much more about who we are connected to than what we are disconnected from. In Chapter 1, we looked at John the Baptist being consecrated to God in the wilder-ness. What made his time in the wilderness so significant was not so much what he was disconnected from but what he was connected to – his passion for the Lord. John was far more captivated by the Lord than he was concerned about any sacrifice and disconnection he may have experienced from temporal pleasures of this world.

Have you found yourself eating from Jezebel's table by watching movies, listening to music or reading books that promote demonic ideologies, sexual immorality or other forms of perversion? Why not take some time to repent before the Lord and ask him to cleanse you of every seed of perversion, deception and darkness that you have allowed into your life. You may want to rededicate your laptop, TV or phone to the Lord. Maybe you need to get rid of some books and magazines that the Lord is highlighting to you. I would also recommend that you pause at this point and take communion as you pray. As you partake of the Lord's table, invite him to change every ungodly appetite in you that's not in alignment with his heart. At the same time, ask the Lord to increase your hunger and desire for his word and his presence.

PART THREE

DEFEATING JEZEBEL

CHAPTER SEVEN

THE SEEKER AND THE SECRET PLACE

Jehu's anointing

I was recently on a trip to northern Nigeria with four friends – a married couple and two guys. We were all travelling from different parts of the UK so the plan was to meet at Heathrow Airport in London. We were scheduled to take a direct flight from Heathrow to Abuja, the capital of Nigeria. On the flight, I was seated with the team leader, the couple was seated a little way away from us, and the fourth team member – let's call him Jonny (not his real name) – was seated in another part of the plane. Everything was going according to plan until about half way through the flight.

An air steward came to us and asked if we were travelling with someone called Jonny. He told us Jonny had fainted, and that he had hit his head and lost about three years of his memory. He basically couldn't remember where he was or where he was going. I couldn't believe my ears. It seemed like something out of a movie. What made this even more concerning for us in the immediate circumstances was that Jonny had a lot of the information for our trip as he was the only one on the team who had been to northern Nigeria before. I remember praying a lot, as well as texting friends and asking them to pray. Thankfully, Jonny's memory returned after a few hours, and following some check-ups on arrival he was fine for the rest of the trip. I've watched movies where people lose their memory and completely forget everything about their identity. Even though my experience on the plane was not that extreme, it was certainly unnerving.

Right after the accident, one of the signs that something was definitely wrong was that Jonny couldn't answer questions about where he was heading. He lost his sense of destiny, so to speak. This incident makes me think about the many people today who are 'air bound', travelling through life, but have no idea of their destiny. Jehu was a biblical character who had a great destiny but was completely blind to it.

Elijah had killed 450 prophets of Baal, called down fire from heaven in the sight of all Israel to prove who the true God was, instigated a spiritual revolution in the nation, but somehow failed to complete the assignment of putting an end to Jezebel's reign. Interestingly, the Lord does not give

Elijah another chance to complete this assignment but rather commands him to anoint three people: Hazael, king over Syria, Jehu, king over Israel, and Elisha as prophet in his place. Elijah only actually ended up anointing Elisha, and delegated the other two anointings to Elisha to perform. Elijah is subsequently taken up into heaven by a whirlwind, while Jezebel's influence continues to grow strong across Israel and Judah.

Although Jezebel wasn't the reigning queen at this time in history, she had positioned her children strategically in both kingdoms. Her son (Joram) was king over Israel and her daughter (Athaliah) was the mother of the king of Judah (Ahaziah). Jezebel was both grandmother to the king of Judah and mother to the king of Israel. In essence, Jezebel was still functioning as the satanic principality over the people of God, and her children were strategically placed in positions of power to implement her evil desires. In the midst of such darkness and spiritual decadence, God raises up a reformer – Jehu!

Jehu was a military commander, who served under Ahab and his son Joram. A mighty man of valour, who was handpicked by God to succeed where Elijah failed, he walked in great authority in his assignment to destroy the stranglehold of Jezebel over the nation. The name Jehu means 'The Lord Is He', and we first hear the Lord mention his name to Elijah in 1 Kings 19. The anointing that was on Jehu caused him to bring about a reformation in the nation. I believe the Lord is releasing this same anointing over his people in these days that we live in.

There are some key things we can learn by taking a closer look at the manner in which the Lord called and anointed Jehu. These lessons are essential for any individual that will be used by God to bring a true reformation as Jehu did.

> Then the Lord said to him: 'Go, return on your way to the Wilderness of Damascus; and when you arrive, anoint Hazael as king over Syria. Also you shall anoint Jehu the son of Nimshi as king over Israel. And Elisha the son of Shaphat of Abel Meholah you shall anoint as prophet in your place. It shall be that whoever escapes the sword of Hazael, Jehu will kill; and whoever escapes the sword of Jehu, Elisha will kill. Yet I have reserved seven thousand in Israel, all whose knees have not bowed to Baal, and every mouth that has not kissed him.'
>
> — 1 Kings 19:15–18

The fact that God was commanding Elijah to anoint Elisha in his place is proof that Elijah's assignment on earth was coming to an end. Biblical scholars believe that Elisha served Elijah for six to eight years before Elijah was taken up to heaven. In his time with Elijah, Elisha must have received the instructions to anoint Hazael king of Syria and Jehu king of Israel. After Elijah was taken up to heaven, it appears to have taken Elisha several more years to get around to anointing Jehu as king of Israel. What I find interesting about this is that the Lord called Jehu by name, prophetically, many years before he was actually anointed. In all those years he was serving under Ahab, and then Joram, as one of the commanders in the army. Jehu had no idea the eye of the Lord was on him as one that would arise to bring a reformation to the nation. The Lord had called him by name – both Elijah and Elisha knew Jehu by name – and yet, all the while, he had no idea these conversations about his destiny had taken place. Jehu would have remained an ordinary commander in the army all his life if not for one of the sons of the prophet declaring to him the word of the Lord over his life. In order for Jehu to step into his assignment, someone had to declare to him who he was called to be.

> And Elisha the prophet called one of the sons of the prophets, and said to him, 'Get yourself ready, take this flask of oil in your hand, and go to Ramoth Gilead. Now when you arrive at that place, look there for Jehu the son of Jehoshaphat, the son of Nimshi, and go in and make him rise up from among his associates, and take him to an inner room. Then take the flask of oil, and pour it on his head, and say, "Thus says the Lord: 'I have anointed you king over Israel.'" Then open the door and flee, and do not delay.'
>
> — 2 Kings 9:1–3

In many ways, Jehu represents a generation on the earth right now that has no idea what the Lord has prepared for them. They don't know that conversations have already taken place between the Lord and his prophets about them and their unique position in his end time agenda for the nations. Like Jehu, many are just 'hanging out' with their friends, with no sense of purpose and vision for their lives. I believe prophetic voices need to arise, like the sons of the prophet who declared to Jehu who he was. These prophetic voices need to begin to release the declaration of identity, purpose and assignment to a generation that is meandering in complacency and addictions, and wasting their lives on things that have no eternal value.

GOD IS SEARCHING

Jehu was specially handpicked by God for this unique assignment. God was searching for a certain type of individual to bring about a reformation in the nation, and clearly Jehu's life met the criteria necessary to carry the anointing to destroy Jezebel, otherwise God would not have picked him. Imagine how many people God vetted before he came to choose Jehu.

When the Lord wants to bring about a revolution and a reformation, he starts by looking for an individual. It's the same way God has worked throughout history. Martin Luther, a German monk, sparked the Protestant Reformation when he nailed *The Ninety-Five Theses* to the door of the church in 1517, and Christianity was forever changed. John Wesley was used mightily by God to bring about a spiritual revolution in Britain and Ireland in the 1700s. William Seymour, Evan

Roberts, Charles Finney are just a few examples of individuals used by the Lord to change their nations. These individuals had the capacity to carry the anointing that was necessary to bring about the move of God in their generation. The fact that God desires to move in a specific way doesn't mean he is always able to find a vessel that can host the dimension of his move that the generation needs. In Isaiah 62, we see a picture of God desiring something but then also making sure there are people on the earth who share the desire for what he wants to do:

> For Zion's sake I will not hold my peace,
> And for Jerusalem's sake I will not rest,
> Until her righteousness goes forth as brightness,
> And her salvation as a lamp that burns.
>
> I have set watchmen on your walls, O Jerusalem;
> They shall never hold their peace day or night.
> You who make mention of the Lord, do not keep silent,
> And give him no rest till he establishes
> And till he makes Jerusalem a praise in the earth.
> — Isaiah 62:1, 6–7

God declares that he will not hold his peace, but then goes on to say that he has set watchmen on the wall who will not hold their peace. If God will not hold his peace, why isn't that enough for Jerusalem to become a praise in the earth? Because, for God to do what he wants to do on earth, he always finds someone on the ground who's in agreement with his desires. Someone who feels what he feels and wants what he wants but who also has the capacity to carry the weight of what he wants to release on the earth. Another scripture that sheds a bit more light on this can be found in the gospel of John.

> But the hour is coming, and now is, when the true wor-
> shippers will worship the Father in spirit and truth; for
> the Father is seeking such to worship him.
>   — John 4:23

Notice, the Father is not just looking for worship but worshippers. The Father is searching for worshippers because worshippers are seekers, and God himself is a seeker. He wants to see a reflection of himself in us. Why would he entrust a dimension of a move of the Spirit to someone who doesn't care about the move of his Spirit like he does? In seeing a reflection of himself in an individual, the Lord finds one who he knows has the same value system for what he is about to release.

Jehu had something in his DNA that was a reflection of the heart of God as it related to his desire to bring judgement on Jezebel. Jehu also possessed the inner fortitude and temperament necessary to bring into manifestation the decreed judgement against Jezebel. Jehu represents a breed of believers that the Lord is raising up to break the hold of Jezebel over a generation, bringing about a spiritual reformation.

This same anointing to destroy the hold of Jezebel is available for us today if only we would prepare ourselves to carry such a reformation anointing.

Let's now look at how God raised Jehu to become an agent of transformation. I believe the same principles apply to us today if we desire to be used by God to break the hold of this spirit of Jezebel over our generation.

THE CALL TO RISE UP

I remember going to a youth camp weekend away in my late teens, with a group of about 150 teenagers in Wales. One of the main speakers at this conference was a man who moved powerfully in the gift of prophecy. In one of his sessions I remember him putting a call out to the whole group and asking anyone who wanted to be used by God to stand up and come forward. I stood up, expecting that most of the room would respond to the call. To my shock and embarrassment, it was just me and one other person that came forward. I really disliked the feeling of standing up there alone, and couldn't understand why none of my friends had responded alongside me. Even though I couldn't fully make sense of it in the moment, I think I knew deep down why they were holding back. They wanted to be 'cool' and seemed more concerned about what others thought about them than what God thought about them. I know God marked my life in a special way when I stood up in that meeting.

Jehu was first made to rise up from among his associates. Jehu was probably very comfortable around his friends, but in order for him to step into what God had for him there needed to be a separation from the crowd. Jehu could not step into what God was calling him into until he was out of what God was calling him out of. Many individuals want to be used by God but are too concerned about fitting in with the crowd.

Negative peer pressure is keeping a lot of people from becoming who God has called them to be – comparing themselves with everyone else around them and trying to fit in with the crowd as opposed to choosing to follow his path for their lives, even if it means standing out. Throughout scripture, it is very clear that the people who end up being used by God to bring about real change in a generation have always been individuals who stood out from the crowd. How else would they have brought a change to the system if they weren't willing to be different?

Although this negative peer pressure is such a strong reality for many people today, I've noticed something strange in my own life: no matter how much I try to 'fit in' I just never quite manage it. God designed me not to fit in but to stand out and be different. If you can relate to this sense of not fitting in, as I'm sure many can, ask yourself this: could this be God's way of getting you to embrace his unique identity and call on your life? Perhaps he is calling you to something bigger than just being one of the crowd.

If you've ever been swimming in a river or the sea you will know that it's a lot easier to go with the flow than it is to swim against the tide. Even a dead fish can float downstream – that doesn't take any effort, strength of character or inner fortitude – but it takes a certain type of fish to swim upstream. God is raising up a Jehu generation that is ready to swim against the tide, stand out from the crowd and usher in a dimension of heaven that brings about reformation on earth.

Jehu being asked to rise up amongst his associates is also a prophetic picture of separation and consecration to God's purposes. Without deep consecration there will be no real elevation into the next dimension. We touched on this principle in Chapter 1, when looking at the life of John the Baptist, and we see this same principle again in God's calling on Jehu, as well as several men and women of God throughout the scriptures and throughout history. Moses was separated for 40 years in the wilderness, Abraham was called out by God to be separated from his father's house unto God's purposes, John the Baptist was in the desert for several years before God made him a voice to change a nation, Samuel was separated from his family to serve the Lord in the temple, Apostle Paul spent time in the Arabian desert being prepared by the Lord himself, Jesus only began his ministry after 40 days of separation in fasting and prayer... Again and again we see that separation is foundational to elevation in the kingdom of God. The Lord desires for us to be separated unto him before we can be effective in working for him.

THE INNER ROOM

After getting Jehu to rise up among his associates, the next instruction was to take him to the inner room. God had found his man, the representative he would use to bring his decrees of judgement on the house of Ahab and Jezebel, but he couldn't get started yet because Jehu wasn't ready. First, he had to get this man to a certain location, 'the inner room', where Jehu would receive a supernatural empowerment (the anointing) to accomplish his God-given assignment.

I have been deeply impacted by the life and ministry of Leonard Ravenhill, an English evangelist and author who focused on the subject of prayer and revival. He once wrote:

> No man is greater than his prayer life. The pastor who is not praying is playing; the people who are not praying are straying. The pulpit can be a shop window to display one's talents; the prayer closet allows no showing off.

The prayer closet truly allows no showing off. Jehu being taken to the inner room is a picture of the prayer closet.

It is also a picture of the secret place, referred to in Psalm 91:1. What happened in this inner room was the secret behind Jehu's success in bringing an end to the reign of Jezebel. The secret place is a place of encounter, a place of safety and a place of revelation. Understanding and embracing the mystery of the secret place is by far the most important element in the

life of any individual that is serious about having an impact
for God in their generation.

> He who dwells in the secret place of the Most High
> Shall abide under the shadow of the Almighty.
>
> — Psalm 91:1

The secret place is the crucial ingredient that brings an individual to a place where they have power with God for a
generation. It is impossible to host dimensions of God that
bring about true revival, revolution and reformation without
having a grasp of this mystery. The inner room is the secret to
the unusual manifestations of the power of God in the lives
of heroes of the faith that we read about in scripture. Moses,
Elijah, Samuel, David, Daniel, the Apostles, and even the Lord
Jesus all had a deep understanding and value for the secret
place. Those who will carry the anointing to bring down
Jezebel in this generation will be those who have mastered
the mystery of the 'inner room'.

The secret place is not a public place, it is a private place.
Notice that Psalm 91 talks about 'He who dwells...', it doesn't
say 'they' or 'them'. This points to the fact that the secret place
is somewhere you go alone; it is not a corporate place. There
are things God will not reveal to you until he gets you alone.

In Genesis 32, Jacob was on his way to meet with his
brother Esau after many years of being apart. Jacob was
afraid and distressed because the last time they were together
he had stolen his brother's blessing, and Esau was planning

on killing him. The night before they reunited, Jacob had an interesting experience:

> And he arose that night and took his two wives, his two female servants, and his eleven sons, and crossed over the ford of Jabbok. He took them, sent them over the brook, and sent over what he had. *Then Jacob was left alone*; and a man wrestled with him until the breaking of day.
> — Genesis 32:22–24 (emphasis added)

This wrestling eventually led to Jacob's name being changed to Israel. However, it only began when Jacob was left alone.

It is often such a battle to get to a place in prayer where you are truly alone. The word 'alone' comes from the combination of two words: 'all' and 'one'. To be alone actually means to be 'all in one'. Have you ever tried to spend time talking and listening to God, but knowing full well that you're not really praying because your mind is so distracted and not really focused on him? This has happened to me many times. To be 'all in one' is to get to a place in prayer where your mind, emotions, body and spirit become one. We can see an example of this in Elijah, when he prayed for rain after three and a half years of drought:

> So Ahab went to eat and drink. But Elijah climbed to the top of Mount Carmel and bowed low to the ground and prayed with his face between his knees.
> — 1 Kings 18:42 (NLT)

Elijah entered this place of oneness when he prayed, and there was a breakthrough as a result. Elijah's physical posture was in alignment with his mind, emotions and spirit. He was fully present and all in one when he prayed for the rain.

I cannot think of any time in my life when I have had a real breakthrough in prayer without this reality of being 'all in one'. I think it is impossible to access the secret place of the Most High without getting to a place of being all in one. Why should God let you access a realm in him that you cannot engage with because you are not ready to let go of a multitude of distractions? We are very often not all in one, even if we are physically alone. To encounter God in a way that brings change to a generation, we have to learn to send everything over the brook, like Jacob did. Many believers have not mastered this, so we never ascend to realms of influence in the spirit that result in generational transformation.

In the realm of the spirit, the secret place is an actual location in God, while in the physical realm it is often connected (but not limited) to a physical location. Teaching on prayer in Matthew 6:6, Jesus says, 'When you pray, go into your room,' but when Elijah stood before Ahab he said, 'As the Lord God of Israel lives before whom I stand there shall not be dew nor rain these years, except at my word.' Elijah was functioning from the secret place, even though he was physically standing before King Ahab. Jesus also functioned from the secret place in the same way – in John 3 we read that he was, like Elijah, functioning in two realms at the same time:

No one has ascended to heaven but he who came down
from heaven, that is, the Son of Man who is in heaven.

— John 3:13

Psalm 91 calls it the secret place of the Most High. The secret
place of the Most High is not your secret place, it is his secret
place. This is one of the reasons why we often find that it's
not easily accessible. There are dimensions in God that are
reserved for the hungry and desperate, and these dimensions
will not and cannot be accessed by a casual pursuit. If an
individual is not intentional and desperate in their pursuit of
his presence, it can be dangerous to bump into God casually.
So, the Lord protects the common gaze by shrouding himself
in a covering of darkness (mystery). In protecting us from
finding him casually he manifests his mercy:

He made darkness his secret place;
His canopy around him was dark waters
And thick clouds of the skies.

— Psalm 18:11

Treasure loses its value if it is easy to get hold of. Similarly, the
jealousy of God causes certain manifestations of his presence
to be hidden from us until all of us seeks all of him. This
should not be confused with the free gift of salvation that is
made available to all. Salvation is free and easily accessible by
whosoever desires eternal life. Although salvation is free, to

grow in depth and maturity in our relationship with the Lord is costly.

If the secret place of the Most High is his secret place and not ours, then how do we get there? The pathway to his secret place is our secret place. The secret place of the Most High is a deep place in the Lord that can only be accessed from an equally deep place in us. In Psalm 42:7 David says, 'Deep calls unto deep at the noise of your waterfalls.' The deep place in us required to access his secret place is actually our secret place. To get there, we have to go into our room (or inner room, in Jehu's case), as Jesus said in Matthew 6:6, and shut the door. This also means getting rid of the distractions and being all in one. When we get to a place where we can be all in one, accessing his secret place becomes a lot easier. Again, it is worth reiterating that shutting the door of a room and being physically on your own does not necessarily mean you are all in one. On the other hand, you can be in a crowd of people with a lot of noise around you but have actually 'shut the door' so that you are all in one, having direct access to his secret place. The secret place is not limited to a geographical location.

The same principles that relate to living from the deep place also operate in the shallow place. Just as deep calls unto deep, shallow calls unto shallow. As soon a person makes the shallow place their 'home' and realm of existence they attract into their lives the things that enable that realm of existence to be their permanent domain.

Those who will carry the anointing necessary to destroy the hold of Jezebel will be people that operate from the secret place. Notice that Psalm 91 says, 'He who dwells...' It doesn't say, 'He who visits the secret place of the Most High.' The secret place has to be our dwelling place. The gravitational pull of his realm has to be so strong that we are completely free from the gravitational pull of the earthly realm. The end result of this will be that we live from heaven to earth and not the other way around. Too many of us are dwelling on earth and visiting the secret place as opposed to dwelling in the secret place and visiting the earth.

In the inner room of Jehu's life-changing encounter were a couple of things that I believe we will also find in our secret place: the word of God and the anointing of God.

A WORD FROM GOD

God speaks in various ways. He is a talking God and has various channels through which he conveys his thoughts and desires to us. Throughout the scriptures, we see that he spoke to individuals in the most peculiar ways. Sometimes it was a still small voice; other times it was an audible voice, thundering from heaven. He also spoke through dreams and visions, through his servants the prophets, and through circumstances.

God still speaks to us today in both simple and dramatic ways, but the written word of God establishes the foundation and the boundaries of God's communication with us. He will not speak a word that contradicts what he has already spoken to us in his written word. In the secret place, Jehu received a word from the Lord (through a prophet) that would change his life forever. It is in the secret place that God begins to give us the strategies, and revelations necessary for fulfilling his calling on our life. The word of God is our source of life. When he speaks, everything changes.

Paul writes, in Romans 10:17, that 'faith comes by hearing, and hearing by the word of God.' The faith Jehu needed to destroy Jezebel came from hearing the word of the Lord in the inner room. When we become a people of the secret place we become a people of his written word, which leads us into encounters with the living Word. The written word of God without the Spirit of God will lead us to be full of information, but no revelation; all theology and no reality. It is possible to become a people of the written word and not of the secret place. There are many people who have an intellectual relationship with the written word, while never encountering the living Word.

The Holy Spirit inspired the different writers of the various books of the Bible to write in ways that concealed the mysteries of God from the enemy. So, in order to understand the Bible we need the Holy Spirit. Even Satan (one of the most intelligent and gifted beings that God ever created) didn't fully understand the scriptures. If he did, he would not have helped God to fulfil his ultimate plan of redemption by crucifying Jesus. Satan did not fully understand the plan of God to bring salvation and redemption to mankind, even though it had already been prophesied. The prophecies could only be understood with the help of the Holy Spirit. In the secret place, we receive the revelation from the Lord that unveils mysteries in the scriptures to us. All of a sudden, the same scripture we have been reading for many years comes alive in a way that we have never before experienced.

Jehu received a word in the secret place that possessed him. The word of the Lord came alive in Jehu and gave him the courage and boldness he needed to execute the Lord's judgement on Jezebel. Those who will carry this Jehu anointing will, in the same way, be people of the word of the Lord.

THE ANOINTING

The other thing that Jehu found in the secret place was the anointing. The anointing is the empowerment from the Holy Spirit that enables us to accomplish supernatural exploits. The Jehu anointing is a warfare anointing: it is militant, it confronts, and it destroys the operation of witchcraft, oppression and perversion.

The young prophet was commanded by Elisha to make Jehu rise from his associates, take him into the inner room and pour the flask of oil (representing the anointing) on his head. The anointing that the young prophet released over Jehu was a compounded anointing, meaning that it was passed down from Elijah to Elisha and then to the young prophet and now to Jehu.

This anointing being passed down to Jehu from several different men of God speaks of the multi-generational nature of what God wants to do in our generation. He is the God of Abraham, Isaac and Jacob. What he starts in one generation he wants to continue in the next. The prophecy in Joel 2:28 about the outpouring of God's Spirit in the last days specifically mentions different generations: the sons and daughters, old men (and women) and young men and women. There is something really special about the different generations working together to advance God's purposes. Jehu was carrying an anointing that came from the Lord, through Elijah:

> Then he arose and went into the house. And he poured the oil on his head, and said to him, 'Thus says the Lord God of Israel: "I have anointed you king over the people of the Lord, over Israel."'
>
> — 2 Kings 9:6

The young prophet first poured the anointing oil on Jehu and then he spoke. The anointing preceded the speaking. In other words, the anointing being released upon Jehu came upon him with a specific assignment, a clear declaration of what it was going to accomplish. Here we have a picture of the word and the Spirit working together. Just as it was in the beginning, when the Spirit of the Lord hovered over the chaos and then God said, 'Let there be light,' the hovering of the Spirit was necessary before the word was released. The word and the Spirit always work together. We don't have to pick one over the other; we need both. As someone once put it: 'the word without the Spirit is dead, and the Spirit without the word is mute.'

> It shall come to pass in that day
> That his burden will be taken away from your shoulder,
> And his yoke from your neck,
> *And the yoke will be destroyed because of the anoint-*
> *ing oil.*
>
> — Isaiah 10:27 (emphasis added)

The yoke of Jezebel over a whole nation could not be confronted without the anointing of the Holy Spirit. Jehu received a yoke-destroying anointing when the son of the prophet poured that oil on him. Looking at Isaiah 10:27, note that the anointing does not just break the yoke but completely destroys it. Something that is broken can be put together again, but when it is destroyed there is no hope of repair.

In the Old Testament, only the priest, the king and the prophet were anointed. However, in the New Testament, all who are born again receive an anointing at new birth. This anointing abides in us for communion and fellowship with the Holy Spirit:

> But the anointing which you have received from him
> *abides in you*, and you do not need that anyone teach
> you; but as the same anointing teaches you concerning

all things, and is true, and is not a lie, and just as it has taught you, you will abide in him.

— 1 John 2:27 (emphasis added)

But you shall receive power when the Holy Spirit has *come upon you*; and you shall be witnesses to me in Jerusalem, and in all Judea and Samaria, and to the end of the earth.

— Acts 1:8 (emphasis added)

Jesus was anointed with the Holy Spirit and anointed with power (Acts 10:38). This enabled him to do good and to heal all who were oppressed by the devil. In Acts 1:8, Jesus tells the disciples that they, too, will be anointed with the Holy Spirit and power. According to 1 John 2:27 there is an anointing that abides in us, but Acts 1:8 speaks of an anointing that comes upon us. I believe these are two ways in which the anointing manifests in the life of a believer: an anointing that comes upon and an anointing that dwells within. The anointing that dwells within is for communion with the Holy Spirit, while the anointing that comes upon is for service.

Both manifestations of the anointing (upon and within) have their source in the secret place. It was in the secret place that Jehu received the anointing upon. However, we see at the end of Jehu's life that even though he was anointed he ended up falling into idolatry:

> However Jehu did not turn away from the sins of
> Jeroboam the son of Nebat, who had made Israel sin,
> that is, from the golden calves that were at Bethel and
> Dan.
>
> — 2 Kings 10:29

If the secret place had become Jehu's dwelling place, there's no way he could have ended up worshipping idols at the end of his life. We should note that the anointing of God on the life of an individual is not a sign of his approval of their behaviour. The way to keep the anointing 'upon' in a place of purity is to grow and guard the anointing 'within'. Both anointings have their source in the secret place, but while the anointing upon can seemingly function for long periods of time without regular contact with the secret place, the anointing within immediately dries up apart from the secret place.

This is why a minister can sometimes appear to be powerfully anointed by God and used in incredible ways and then we later find out that they were engaging in a sinful lifestyle, even while the Lord was apparently using them. A part of the problem is that we often use external manifestations of the anointing of God on our lives as a gauge of the depth of our relationship with him. This is a major pitfall for many minsters of the gospel. Moving in the gifts of the Spirit is not a sign of spiritual maturity or depth of intimacy with the Lord.

There are individuals in the body of Christ who are living in sin, but somehow they still appear anointed. As a result of this, they end up in self-deception and sometimes inadvertently partnering with a demonic spirit. They started in the spirit but ended in the flesh, because they were too focused on the anointing upon them and lost sight of the anointing within. When the anointing upon you becomes heavier than the anointing within you, it ends up crushing you. As children of God, we want to grow in the anointing upon us for effective ministry, but we must never neglect the anointing within. We must always make sure we are functioning from the secret place, otherwise we are heading for shipwreck. One of the signs that an individual has not been in the secret place for a long time is pride. When we meet God in the secret place, there are certain things he will not allow us to take back with us. God has a way of using the secret place to strengthen our spirit and weaken our flesh.

Just as Jehu was anointed in the secret place, the Lord is raising up a new breed of believers who will make the secret place their dwelling place, and as a result they will be entrusted with anointings that will bring deliverance to a generation under the spell of witchcraft and Jezebel. This new breed of believers that the Lord is raising up will not have their identity tied to the anointing upon them for service but will be rooted in the anointing of intimacy with God as their foundational identity.

As we have seen, Jehu was identified by God a long time before he became aware of it. He had no idea the eye of the Lord was on him as one that would arise to bring about a reformation in the nation, until a prophet declared it to him. I thank God for prophets! The prophetic gift is a revelatory gift that unveils the mind of God to us. However, you don't need to wait for a prophet to declare to you who God has called you to be before you begin to walk in this calling. It's nice when that happens, but I love the scripture in 1 Corinthians 2:9 that says, 'Eye has not seen, nor ear heard, nor have entered into the heart of man the things which God has prepared for those who love him. But God has revealed them to us through his Spirit.' God wants to reveal to you what he has prepared for you. I believe God wants you to live with a full awareness of what he has put you on the earth for.

Jehu had to rise up from amongst his companions, he had to stand out from the crowd. Are you willing to stand out from the crowd and be different? Those who will be used by God to overthrow the spirit of Jezebel will be people who are more concerned about what God has to say about them than about what others are thinking. Jehu was first separated from his companions and then elevated to a new position of authority that resulted in him spearheading a revolution.

The inner room was where everything changed for Jehu. He had an encounter in the secret place and was a different man when he came out. When did you last have an encounter with God in your secret place? In Jehu's secret place he found the living Word and the anointing. These two working together in our lives make us an unstoppable force for good, destroying the influence of Jezebel and advancing the purposes of heaven on earth.

CHAPTER EIGHT

THE FIRE AND
THE FURY

Jehu's battle

In May 2017, I was spending time preparing for an upcoming Prayer Storm gathering in Manchester. The nature of these prayer gatherings follows the model of 2 Chronicles 7:14. As God's people, we cannot see a healing of the land without first humbling ourselves, praying, seeking his face and turning from our own wicked ways. We always have repentance and consecration to God as a foundation for our prayers of intercession over the nation. There is no point gathering the Church to seek God for transformation and reformation in our nation if we ourselves are married to the idols of the land. There needs to be repentance and a turning away from our own wicked ways first, before we can see our prayers for a move of God in the nation become a reality.

With this in mind, I was preparing and praying, asking the Lord what he wanted me to speak about at the start of the day. I knew that sexual immorality in the body of Christ was something the Lord wanted us to address during this gathering, and my attention was drawn to the story of Jehu. For the first time, I caught a glimpse of how the Lord would destroy the hold of Jezebel over our generation. My mind was completely blown away! When I shared these simple truths that I am about to share with you at our prayer gathering the following day, there was great deliverance from the influence of the spirit of Jezebel in the lives of those gathered in that place.

In the previous chapter, we explored how Jehu received his anointing. The nation of Israel was about to experience a monumental change because of one man's encounter in the inner room. This encounter was so significant that it would bring about a spiritual reformation. The magnitude of the assignment required a messenger with such a depth of encounter that it produced an anointing capable of bringing about a revolution. We should never underestimate the power of an encounter with God. Until we become a people who have truly encountered God and live from the place of that encounter, we will not have the authority to bring about a reformation in our nation.

> Then Jehu came out to the servants of his master, and
> one said to him, 'Is all well? Why did this madman
> come to you?' And he said to them, 'You know the
> man and his babble.' And they said, 'A lie! Tell us now.'
> So he said, 'Thus and thus he spoke to me, saying,
> "Thus says the Lord: 'I have anointed you king over
> Israel.'"' Then each man hastened to take his garment
> and put it under him on the top of the steps; and they
> blew trumpets, saying, 'Jehu is king!'
>
> — 2 Kings 9:11–13

In this passage, when Jehu comes out of the inner room he
tries to downplay his meeting with the prophet. However, his
friends somehow sense that he isn't telling the truth. How did
they know that he was attempting to deceive them? Perhaps
they saw traces of the anointing oil on his head and clothes?
Or could it be that the encounter in the inner room had such
an effect on Jehu that he wasn't able to conceal it? It is impossible to have an encounter with God and not be transformed.
It is also impossible to have an encounter with God and for it
to escape the notice of the people who know you.

How is it possible that many claim to have encountered
God but continue to live lives that don't remotely come close
to that of a person who has experienced intimacy with the
God who created the universe? Could it be that many are
living in the memory of yesterday's passion and not the reality
of today's fire? Or could it be that we are settling for the
smoke, rather than going after the fire itself? When we have

encountered the fire of God it should be obvious to those close to us because fire does not need to be advertised; it speaks for itself. As Leonard Ravenhill once said, 'The reason the world is going to hell fire tonight is because the church has lost Holy Ghost Fire.'

We need a fresh encounter with God. Before the encounter in the inner room Jehu was simply another commander in the army, but after the encounter he was anointed to be king and his companions had to radically change their perception of him. This is what happens when we encounter God: those who knew us beforehand will have to adjust their perceptions of us because we are obviously and tangibly changed.

The moment Jehu's companions were told the details of the prophetic word, they quickly put their garments under him and blew the trumpet, declaring him king. It's amazing to me that these companions weren't envious of his new-found status, and that they made no attempt to undermine the prophetic word. They perceived the anointing on Jehu, even though they didn't witness the act for themselves. This suggests to me that Jehu surrounded himself with some really good friends, who were not intimidated by his promotion. It is also striking that Jehu was declared king by the prophetic word but he didn't declare himself king; others saw what was on him and blew the trumpet. The position of influence that came to Jehu was not reached by self-promotion. Too many people are trying to step into positions of influence by self-promotion because they lack the patience to go through God's process.

Abraham, the father of faith, made some mistakes in his walk with God that provide powerful lessons for us today, and one of them was all about patience. The Lord had promised to make him a great nation, but both he and Sarah were in their old age and had no children. In frustration from waiting for so long for the promise to be realised, Sarah persuaded Abraham to sleep with her servant Hagar in the hope that he would be able to build a family this way. As a result, Hagar gave birth to Ishmael. Years later, God did indeed fulfil his promise to Abraham and Sarah by giving them a son, Isaac. So Ishmael was a product of impatience and a work of the flesh, while Isaac was a product of faith and doing things God's way. When we are impatient with God's process and decide to go it alone, we end up birthing Ishmaels rather than receiving the promise of Isaac.

Having been through God's process, Jehu was receiving the 'promise'. God had promoted Jehu and made a way for him to step into this position and no one was going to stop it. Jehu's companions respond to his encounter in the inner room:

> Then each man hastened to take his garment and put
> it under him on the top of the steps; and they blew
> trumpets, saying, 'Jehu is king!'
>
> — 2 Kings 9:13

Jehu's companions put their garments under him. This was an incredible display of honour; a recognised act of homage to a king. Conversely, in the book of Genesis we read how Joseph's brothers greatly resented him when he shared his dream with them. Their hatred led them to sell Joseph into slavery, taking his coat and dipping it in blood to deceive their father into believing he was dead.

> Joseph had a dream, and when he told it to his brothers, they hated him all the more. He said to them, 'Listen to this dream I had: We were binding sheaves of grain out in the field when suddenly my sheaf rose and stood upright, while your sheaves gathered around mine and bowed down to it.' His brothers said to him, 'Do you intend to reign over us? Will you actually rule us?' And they hated him all the more because of his dream and what he had said.
>
> — Genesis 37:5–8

What made them hate him even more was the idea that his dream suggested that he would reign over them. Here's an interesting contrast: on the one hand you have a group of commanders, colleagues and equals, and when one of them is unexpectedly promoted to be king the others immediately take off their garments to lay them on the step for their new ruler; and on the other hand you have a group of brothers who are so jealous of their kid brother reigning over them that they end up selling him into slavery and stripping him of his coat. Jehu's colleagues took off their coats for him, while Joseph's brothers took his coat from him. Jehu's colleagues were more like brothers who supported one another, while Joseph's brothers were more like colleagues who competed with one another.

Too many believers get jealous of one another and (usually, figuratively!) throw each other into pits rather than celebrating and honouring one another – especially when God seems to promote someone above us who we see as a colleague and an equal. If Jehu was among us today – a neighbour or a colleague – and the Lord spoke in the way he did, I wonder if the reaction would be the same. Jehu's friends knew that since he had just received the word of the Lord and had also been anointed it could mean only one thing: Jezebel's reign was over. They all shared a common enemy and did not so much care about who got the credit for bringing her down as long as her influence was completely eradicated. This is a picture of the amazing things that can be achieved 'when no one cares who takes the credit,' as Harry Truman is believed to have said. It is so important for the Church to come together in humility and unity to support individuals whom God is highlighting as 'Jehus': those who are anointed to bring about reformation in our culture. This is vital if we are going to have the kind of impact we are called to have on earth as the body of Christ.

Where was Jehu when Jezebel was killing the prophets? Where was Jehu when Elijah ran away from Jezebel? Where was Jehu when the people of God were being deceived and worshipping Baal? We don't know. He wasn't on the scene just yet because his day of manifestation had not arrived.

Jehu was being prepared for many years, behind the scenes, for a *kairos* moment, and the moment had now come. Now was the fullness of time, his time to come to the forefront. His character and charisma collided with *kairos* and the end result was a convergence. Jehu was caught up in a prophetic whirlwind, and he was unstoppable.

IS IT PEACE?

Possessed by a word, anointed with oil and burning with a zeal to execute the vengeance of the Lord, Jehu rides his chariot to Jezreel:

> Now a watchman stood on the tower in Jezreel, and he saw the company of Jehu as he came, and said, 'I see a company of men.' And Joram said, 'Get a horseman and send him to meet them, and let him say, "Is it peace?"' So the horseman went to meet him, and said, 'Thus says the king: "Is it peace?"' And Jehu said, 'What have you to do with peace? Turn around and follow me.' So the watchman reported, saying, 'The messenger went to them, but is not coming back.' Then he sent out a second horseman who came to them, and said, 'Thus says the king: "Is it peace?"' And Jehu answered, 'What have you to do with peace? Turn around and follow me.'
>
> — 2 Kings 9:17–19

Watchmen were positioned on the highest part of the city wall and it was their job to spot anything that was approaching the city and warn the people of any danger. Here, the watchman spots Jehu and his company. Clearly Jehu was not alone; he was probably riding with the same group of commanders that blew the trumpet and declared him king.

The watchman then reports to Joram, king of Israel, what he sees. Two horsemen were successively sent out to Jehu's company and they were told to ask, 'Is it peace?' What an interesting question, coming from a king who was the son of Jezebel. The 'peace' he was referring to was, though, a false peace. The reign and influence of Jezebel through her son and grandson had brought such an atmosphere of oppression over the people of God, and they had been under her influence for so long that many things that should be considered abnormal were now accepted as part of every day life. Oppression was the new normal, and depression, Baal worship and immorality were nothing to raise an eyebrow at. If the answer to Joram's question – 'Is it peace?' – was yes, then the status quo would have just continued.

But Jehu was challenging the status quo. Often, people think that maintaining the status quo is a way of 'keeping the peace', when what the Lord wants to do is to completely eradicate the status quo (false peace) and bring about true freedom. For far too long, the people of God had been cohabiting with the enemy they were called to evict and now Jehu was anointed by God to declare war! As Aristotle put it, 'We make war that we may live in peace.'

The horsemen responded to Jehu by following him, and there are a couple of possible explanations for this: either they were scared and knew they had no chance of defying his order, or they agreed with him and were glad to finally be challenging the influence of Jezebel over their nation. I believe it is more likely that they joined Jehu's rebellion against Jezebel out of a sense of agreement with Jehu's purpose as opposed joining him for fear of losing their lives.

I like to think that Jehu was a breath of fresh air to these messenger horsemen. They had been under the oppression of Jezebel and her children for so long that they were probably relieved someone was finally going to do something about it. Sometimes people can be under such an atmosphere of oppression that they completely forget what it's like to be free. A fish in water doesn't know it's wet because that's all it has ever known. The anointing on Jehu empowered people to rise above the status quo. The people of this generation who will carry an anointing, like Jehu, to bring about a reformation will also have a strong leadership anointing: they will not be afraid to challenge the status quo, and they will empower those around them to rise up and do the same.

The word of the Lord to Elijah in 1 Kings 19:17 was this: 'It shall be that whoever escapes the sword of Hazael, Jehu will kill; and whoever escapes the sword of Jehu, Elisha will kill.' Joram and Ahaziah had both escaped the sword of Hazael and now the next part of the prophecy was about to be fulfilled. There was going to be no peace for these kings; what awaited them was death. This is echoed in Jesus' declaration about Jezebel's children in Revelation 2:23: 'I will kill her children with death, and all the churches shall know that I am he who searches the minds and hearts...'

THE DRIVING OF JEHU

One of the most important things in warfare is the element of surprise. Jehu and his company had the upper hand in this battle because they had caught the two kings off guard. It would have taken a long time for the approaching army to get close enough to Jezreel for the watchman to recognise who was leading it.

> So the watchman reported, saying, 'He went up to them and is not coming back; and the driving is like the driving of Jehu the son of Nimshi, for *he drives furiously*!'
>
> — 2 Kings 9:20 (emphasis added)

For the watchman on the wall to have recognised it was Jehu just by the way he drove the chariot tells us that Jehu clearly had a reputation as a furious driver. The Hebrew word for 'he drives furiously' comes from the same root as 'madman'. And remember that the messenger (one of the sons of the prophet) who delivered the prophetic word to Jehu and anointed him in the inner room was referred to as a madman. The anointing to execute judgement on Jezebel manifested on the young prophet as 'madness' and this word also means 'fierce' and 'fury'. When Jehu received this anointing it manifested on him in the same way: just as the young prophet was called a madman, so also was Jehu.

The phrase 'he drives furiously' reminds me of Jesus' comment on the life of John the Baptist:

> And from the days of John the Baptist until now the kingdom of heaven suffers violence, and the violent take it by force.
>
> — Matthew 11:12

Jehu was a foreshadow of this revelation of spiritual violence that John the Baptist modelled. There is a holy anger that comes with the anointing that destroys the yoke of Jezebel off a generation.

Imagine you are trying to swim upstream against the flow of a river: if you do nothing, by default you will be swept away. If you try to swim upstream and the force you are applying is equal to the force of the river downstream, you won't go anywhere. To make any real progress upstream, you have to apply a force that is far greater than that which is coming against you downstream. This is what Jesus meant when he said, 'the violent take it by force.' In other words, only the spiritually violent are able to make significant progress upstream. By using the phrase 'spiritually violent' I refer to wholeheartedness in devotion to the Lord. It is choosing not to settle for anything less than God's best in the area of intimacy with him. Such a disposition is violent in the spirit against distraction, compromise or sin.

Too many Christians are being swept away with the current because there is no spiritual violence in their lives. The spirit of Jezebel has infiltrated their lives and they are not aware of it, just like the fish in water that doesn't know it's wet. If you don't consciously stand against the spirit of Jezebel you will be subconsciously influenced by it.

Many believers are casual about their relationship with God and the subtle attacks of the enemy to silence their voice and neutralise their authority. I have come to realise from personal experience that if all I do is go to church on a Sunday morning, and maybe a midweek service, by default I back-slide in my relationship with God. The opposition is so great against the purposes of God in our generation that the default position of doing nothing will lead us to be swept away in the wave of delusion, oppression, and perversion. To overthrow the spirit of Jezebel in our culture we need to be radical in our devotion to the Lord and on fire for God, as John the Baptist was. Spiritual violence, or riding furiously as it was with Jehu, is manifested in a radical devotion to the Lord in prayer and fasting, and zero tolerance for sin and compromise.

As we saw in Chapter 4, although Queen Jezebel was killed, the demonic spirit that she hosted in her body and gave full expression to through her lifestyle (that which we now call the 'spirit of Jezebel') actually pre-dated her:

Now Israel remained in Acacia Grove, and the people
began to *commit harlotry* with the women of Moab.
They invited the people to the *sacrifices of their gods*,
and the *people ate* and bowed down to their gods. So
Israel was joined to Baal of Peor, and the anger of the
Lord was aroused against Israel.

— Numbers 25:1–3 (emphasis added)

This is the first time in the Bible that we read of the children of
Israel being seduced into Baal worship. Here we see the same
issues that later manifested under the reign of Queen Jezebel:
sexual immorality, idol worship, sacrifices and eating things
sacrificed to idols. These were also the same issues Jesus raised
with the church in Thyatira. So here we have three timelines:
before Jezebel, during her reign, and after Jezebel. Three different timelines in history, but all manifestations of the same
spirit with the same traits.

As a result of the children of Israel joining themselves to
Baal with sexual immorality and the eating of things sacrificed to idols, the anger of the Lord was aroused against Israel
and a plague was released. In the midst of the congregation,
while many were weeping before the tabernacle of meeting
because of their sin, one of the men of Israel had the audacity
to present a Midianite woman (the very women that had
lured the men into immorality). Phinehas responded to this
display of rebellion with a violent act, which brought an end
to the plague, and the Lord rewarded him in return.

Now when Phinehas the son of Eleazar, the son of
Aaron the priest, saw it, he rose from among the congregation and took a javelin in his hand; and he went
after the man of Israel into the tent and thrust both
of them through, the man of Israel, and the woman
through her body. So the plague was stopped among
the children of Israel.

— Numbers 25:7–8

Then the Lord spoke to Moses, saying: 'Phinehas the
son of Eleazar, the son of Aaron the priest, has turned
back my wrath from the children of Israel, because
he was zealous with my zeal among them, so that
I did not consume the children of Israel in my zeal.
Therefore say, "Behold, I give to him my covenant of
peace."'

— Numbers 25:10–12

The manner in which Phinehas brought an end to the plague
was undoubtedly violent. Again, this was a foreshadow of the
spiritual violence required to bring an end to the influence of
the spirit of Jezebel that had made Baal worship the official
state religion of the people of God. What we see with Phinehas
and the spirit that rested on him is exactly what we see with
Jehu when he rode furiously. This is also the same spirit that
rested on John the Baptist, causing Jesus to use his life as a
template of what spiritual violence looks like in advancing
the kingdom of God. The spirit of Jezebel only understands

the language of spiritual violence. As someone once said, 'You can't defeat your demons if you're still enjoying their company.' There has to be a holy anger arising in the heart of the people of God that says enough is enough, no more compromise and tolerance of the spirit of Jezebel. It comes down now!

BATTLE AT THE GATE

After being identified by the watchman on the wall, Jehu proceeded to kill both King Joram and King Ahaziah, who were the offspring of Jezebel and the extension of her rule as a principality in the nations of Israel and Judah. He continued to ride his chariot and would not stop until the assignment was complete and Jezebel was dethroned.

> Now when Jehu had come to Jezreel, Jezebel heard of it; and she put paint on her eyes and adorned her head, and looked through a window. Then, as Jehu entered at the gate, she said, 'Is it peace, Zimri, murderer of your master?'
>
> — 2 Kings 9:30–31

We talked earlier about the eye gate and the ear gate being major entry points for the spirit of Jezebel to influence our lives. Here, we see that Jehu arrives at the gate. This really sets the scene for the battle that's about to take place. Jehu was taking the battle to Jezebel's gate, but she was also about to launch major attacks at his 'gates'. This was going to be a battle of the 'gates' at the gate.

It is interesting to note that, previously, Elijah lost the battle to Jezebel at the gate. John the Baptist also lost his head because the spirit of Jezebel (working through Herodias' daughter) captured Herod's gates through seductive dance. Winning the battle at the gate is absolutely key in overcoming Jezebel. Let's take a look at how and why Elijah lost the battle at the gate.

ELIJAH'S BATTLE AT THE GATE

Elijah had just declared to Ahab that he should go home and eat because he could hear the sound of an abundance of rain. While Ahab went on his way, Elijah went to the top of Mount Carmel and began to pray for the rain. After he had a breakthrough in prayer and saw a cloud the size of a man's hand, the hand of the Lord came on Elijah.

> Then the hand of the Lord came upon Elijah; and he girded up his loins and ran ahead of Ahab to the entrance of Jezreel. And Ahab told Jezebel all that Elijah had done, also how he had executed all the prophets with the sword. Then Jezebel sent a messenger to Elijah, saying, 'So let the gods do to me, and

> more also, if I do not make your life as the life of one
> of them by tomorrow about this time.'
> — 1 Kings 18:46, 1 Kings 19:1–2

It appears that when Elijah got to the entrance of Jezreel, he stayed there and did nothing. Why would the hand of the Lord come so powerfully upon Elijah that he outran a chariot only to get to the gate of Jezreel (Jezebel's headquarters) and do nothing? Earlier, Elijah had summoned Ahab to gather the 850 prophets of Baal and Asherah, but only the 450 prophets of Baal showed up on Mount Carmel. The prophets of Baal were not able to call down fire from heaven after hours of calling on their god. Elijah called down fire from heaven after a short and simple prayer and then ordered the execution of the prophets of Baal. After executing the 450 prophets of Baal, Elijah's intention must have been to execute the remaining 400 prophets of Asherah, and Jezebel. For Elijah to have suddenly stopped at the gate of Jezreel, something strange must have happened to him. Jezebel's words to Elijah were more than just threatening speech; they were pregnant with demonic powers that somehow managed to influence Elijah. How could a man who spoke so boldly, called down fire from heaven and moved in incredible supernatural power end up praying to God that he might die?

> But he himself went a day's journey into the wilderness, and came and sat down under a broom tree. And he prayed that he might die, and said, 'It is enough!

Now, Lord, take my life, for I am no better than my fathers!'

— 1 Kings 19:4

The Bible doesn't explain what happened but I am convinced that Jezebel used her powers of witchcraft against Elijah. We know she operated in witchcraft (2 Kings 9:22) so it's certainly plausible. My guess is that after the great exploits on Mount Carmel, Elijah must have been emotionally vulnerable and maybe physically tired as well. This could have been an entry point for Jezebel to strike with her witchcraft, resulting in fear, intimidation and demonic depression. Elijah was now feeling suicidal.

I understand that depression is not always a result of demonic oppression and that there are individuals who suffer from depression as a result of chemical imbalances in the brain. However, in my experience with depression, what I went through mentally and emotionally in those moments of oppression was definitely not caused by a chemical imbalance. You cannot medicate demons; you have to cast them out of your life!

I have noticed that some of the times I have experienced demonic depression have been soon after a major breakthrough in my life, where I have seen God move and use me in incredible ways to impact the lives of many people. There have been times when I have just had to force myself to declare the word of God, even when everything in me fought against it. Many times, I have gone against my feelings and emotions, and I have experienced almost instant breakthroughs.

Jezebel couldn't kill Elijah, and she knew it. To have sent a messenger directly to Elijah, Jezebel must have known where he was. As king and queen of Israel, she and Ahab could have sent soldiers to arrest him or strike him down. I guess they knew he could call down fire from heaven so maybe that was a deterrent! Regardless, Jezebel was really scared of Elijah and knew she couldn't physically kill him so she made him want to do it to himself. He wanted to die. This is the same principle Jesus refers to in the book of Revelation as the doctrine of Balaam (Numbers 22-24). Balaam knew he couldn't curse the people of God so he got them to put a curse on themselves by seducing them into immorality with the Moabite women. What Jezebel couldn't do to Elijah, she planted in his mind to do to himself – it was like a self-imposed curse:

> Then Jezebel sent a messenger to Elijah, saying, 'So let the gods do to me, and more also, if I do not make your life as the life of one of them by tomorrow about this time.' *And when he saw that*, he arose and ran for his life, and went to Beersheba, which belongs to Judah, and left his servant there.
>
> — 1 Kings 19:2–3 (emphasis added)

The messenger came with words for Elijah from Jezebel, but when Elijah 'saw that' he ran for his life. Here we see that Jezebel engaged both Elijah's ear gate and eye gate. This was her way of hijacking his mind. Once his mind had been hijacked, the next thing was for his mouth to birth what the enemy had conceived in his mind. Elijah could not possess the gate of Jezebel because Jezebel had possessed his gates. In Chapter 5, we looked at the importance of having strict security checks at the eye gate and ear gate if we don't want our minds hijacked by the enemy. Sadly, Elijah lost the battle to Jezebel because she was able to get through his gates. Her weapons and venom against him were fear, intimidation, manipulation, deception and depression. She got in through his eye and ear gate. Her weapons against the prophetic move of God are still the same today.

JEHU'S BATTLE AT THE GATE

Riding furiously on his horse, having killed Jezebel's grandson (Ahaziah, king of Judah) and Jezebel's son (Joram, king of Israel), Jehu takes the battle to Jezebel's gate:

> Now when Jehu had come to Jezreel, Jezebel heard of it; and she put paint on her eyes and adorned her head, and looked through a window. Then, as Jehu entered at the gate, she said, 'Is it peace, Zimri, murderer of your master?' And he looked up at the window, and said, 'Who is on my side? Who?' So two or three eunuchs looked out at him.
>
> — 2 Kings 9:30–32

Jezebel was informed that Jehu was in town and that he had killed both her son and grandson. She didn't seem to mourn their deaths but rather focused on beautifying herself because she was actually preparing herself for war. Her strategy this time around was different to the one she had used against Elijah. Her every move was calculated to inflict maximum damage. Why would she beautify herself for Jehu, when she was probably old enough to be his mother, or even grandmother? I think it's because she was looking to seduce him. From a natural standpoint, Jehu could not have been attracted to Jezebel, but there was a supernatural power at work in her eyes. If Jehu engaged those eyes he would be bewitched and fall into her trap. Seduction is spiritual. Her target was his eye gate and she was projecting lust. Here we see the spirit of Jezebel at work, doing what she does best.

Amazingly, even as she projected lust, Jehu did not engage Jezebel's eyes. This is a picture of what society is like today. The spirit of Jezebel is constantly projecting lust through movies, music videos, billboard adverts, fashion, and so on. Her target is the eye gate, with the aim of hijacking our minds. Like Jehu, we may not be able to stop Jezebel from projecting lust and perversion but our job is to make sure that we don't engage her. Much like the dream the Lord gave me about Medusa's head (in Chapter 3), those who engage with its eyes are turned to stone. We live in a sexually charged culture, where pornography is very easily accessible. In fact, everything is so sexualised and this has become such an accepted norm that we don't even really have to go looking for pornography; it is more like pornography comes looking for us. This is a strategy of the spirit of Jezebel to possess the eye gate of a generation. The spirit behind pornography is Jezebel; it is a spirit of lust and seduction. Even though the enemy is continually projecting seduction and perversion, it is our responsibility not to engage.

Several times throughout this book, I have quoted the prophecy of the outpouring of God's Spirit on all flesh. I believe the enemy is terrified of this prophecy:

> And it shall come to pass in the last days, says God,
> That I will pour out of My Spirit on all flesh;
> Your sons and your daughters shall prophesy,
> Your young men shall see visions,
> Your old men shall dream dreams.
>
> — Acts 2:17

Dreams and visions are the language of the Holy Spirit in the last days. Dreams and visions engage the mind. The enemy knows this and has therefore made it very difficult for this generation to have pure imaginations by sexualising the world we live in. Jesus said that whoever looks at a woman with lust for her has already committed adultery with her in his heart. So, as far as Jesus is concerned, your imagination is reality to him. Perhaps this is why the Bible says the pure in heart will see God (Matthew 5:8). Your purity of heart causes your eye gate to have access to realms of glory. The reverse is also true: guarding the purity of your eye gate causes your heart to ascend into realms of glory.

The spirit of Jezebel attacks the eye because it is one of the major gateways to the heart. Her goal is to contaminate the mind, making it impossible for an individual to engage with the true language of the Spirit in these last days. Imagine I had a bottle of pure water and wanted to pour it into a glass. If the glass is dirty on the inside, it really doesn't matter how pure the water is; the moment it gets into the glass it becomes contaminated.

The answer to Jezebel's attack on the eye gate is to behold the Lamb of God, who takes away the sins of the world. The revelation of Jesus to the church that is plagued by sexual immorality is the revelation of his fiery eyes (Revelation 2:18). When your eyes truly catch his fiery gaze, you find the influence of Jezebel destroyed over your life and that lust cannot remain in your heart. The fire in his eyes is meant to become a reality in your eyes, with the end result being a transformed life. The presence of lust in your heart is a sign of the absence of his fire in your eyes. You are transformed by what you gaze upon.

Once Jezebel realised Jehu wasn't engaging with the projection and seduction from her eyes, she switched tactics to engage his ear gate. She said, 'Is it peace, Zimri, murderer of your master?' This was a loaded question. She knew he wasn't coming in peace and she knew he had just killed Joram and Ahaziah. Why would she even think to try to engage his

ears by asking if he came in peace? The 'peace' Jezebel wanted
was one of tolerating her: a 'peace' of keeping the status quo.

Jesus challenged the church of Thyatira that they tolerated
Jezebel (Revelation 2:20). Basically, they came into agreement
with her false peace. It's a peace where she is never challenged
and everyone around her is a 'yes man' or 'yes woman'. This
tolerance is the false peace that Jezebel wants Jehu and the
nation to live under.

I find it interesting that God gave Phinehas a covenant
of peace because of an act of violence, ending the plague of
judgement on the nation (Numbers 25). It was a covenant of
peace because Phinehas' act had brought peace between God
and the nation. Jehu was on his way to perform a similar act of
peace-building between God and the nation. Recognising the
anointing on Jehu, Jezebel starts by challenging his mission to
bring true peace by mockingly offering false peace. Observe
that the Israelite that Phinehas killed as he turned the wrath
of God away from the nation was also called Zimri (son of
Salu – Numbers 25:14).

Jezebel calling Jehu 'Zimri, murderer of your master' was
her way of mocking him in an attempt to get into his heart.
She was referring to a different Zimri, though (servant of
Elah, king of Israel – 1 Kings 16:9–20). This Zimri holds the
record for the king with the shortest reign in Israel's history.
He was king for seven days, and then he committed suicide
by burning the palace over himself. Zimri had murdered the
previous king, who was his master, so his name became syn-
onymous with anyone who was a traitor (much like the way

that the name Judas is often used today to refer to anyone who betrays a friend). However, I think something deeper was going on here when Jezebel called Jehu by Zimri's name. The manner in which Zimri died was suicide, and the effect of Jezebel's witchcraft on Elijah was suicidal thoughts. So here I think she was attempting to hijack Jehu's mind and bring him to a place of depression and suicide, and her pathway to achieve this was to get in through his ear gate. Jehu wasn't having any of it. He could now possess Jezebel's gate because she failed to possess his.

Just as Jezebel attempted to hijack Jehu's mind by getting through his eye gate with lust, and through his ear gate with intimidation, mockery, depression and suicidal thoughts, this is how she continues to operate today. She failed to engage Jehu's gates because he did not have any inward tolerance of her, he was on fire (spiritual violence), he operated from the secret place, he was anointed, he was possessed by the word of the Lord and he had high security at his gates.

CHAPTER NINE

THE EUNUCHS

Jehu's unexpected allies

While preparing for our Prayer Storm gathering back in May of 2017, I felt the Lord ask me, 'James, who killed Jezebel?' I was surprised. I had always thought the answer was pretty straightforward: Jehu killed Jezebel. But as I looked at the passage again, I was shocked to find that it wasn't Jehu who dealt the deadly blow; it was the eunuchs!

As we have seen, the anointing on Jehu empowered others around him to rise above the status quo. This anointing of empowerment caused the messengers from King Joram to join his company in resisting Jezebel's rule as he drove his chariot towards Jezreel. When Jezebel tried to engage Jehu's eyes and ears he totally ignored her. Instead, looking up at the window, he empowered the eunuchs to rise up and break their agreement with Jezebel's false peace so that they could throw her down. In a surprising turn of events, the individuals closest to Jezebel, consecrated to serve her agenda, became Jehu's unexpected allies in bringing about her destruction:

> And he [Jehu] looked up at the window, and said, 'Who is on my side? Who?' So two or three eunuchs looked out at him. Then he said, 'Throw her down.' So they threw her down, and some of her blood spattered on the wall and on the horses; and he trampled her underfoot.
>
> — 2 Kings 9:32–33

Who are these eunuchs? Well, in history, a eunuch was a man whose job it was to guard the bedroom door of a royal woman in order to protect her. These guards were castrated to make them less threatening to the women they guarded. The kings of Israel and Judah imitated their royal neighbours in employing eunuchs in military and other official posts.

When Jehu looked at these eunuchs guarding Jezebel, I believe the very anointing that was poured on him by the young prophet (who was described as a madman), that caused him to ride his chariot with such fury, was now the same anointing that somehow came upon the eunuchs and prompted them to take the bold and defiant act of throwing Jezebel down. How could they have gone from guarding Jezebel one moment to throwing her down the next? Maybe they too were tired of her reign but felt trapped and powerless against her, until Jehu showed up? Or perhaps they were under such deception and oppression due to Jezebel's witchcraft that this 'madman' or breaker anointing on Jehu brought instant deliverance to them through his words. Words that, by the way, they received through their ear gate and eye gate – the very channels through which Jezebel had oppressed Elijah and had tried to influence Jehu. Regardless, I am convinced that whatever happened to the eunuchs that led them to throw Jezebel down had to be supernatural.

The eunuchs were the closest people to Jezebel, and they would have had first hand experience of her oppressive, domineering and intimidating personality. All their lives they had been under her rule with no idea that they were the ones destined to bring an end to her reign. All they needed was a Jehu coming from the secret place carrying the holy fire of God to empower them to do what they were destined to do: throw Jezebel down!

Jehu was commissioned by the Lord to avenge the blood of the prophets and all the servants of the Lord that was shed at the hand of Jezebel, and the eunuchs played a vital role in executing Jehu's mission. The eunuchs were one of God's hidden weapons in dethroning Jezebel. Even though they had been consecrated to serving her agenda, God was going to use them to fulfil prophecy. Little did they know the significant role they would play in bringing about a reformation in the nation. The eunuchs cannot and should not be under-estimated or ignored; just as they were pivotal in the days of Jehu in destroying Jezebel, so also they now will play a vital role in destroying the influence of Jezebel over a generation.

I believe the manner in which Jezebel was dethroned gives us a prophetic template of how the Lord will bring destruction on this spirit in these last days.

I felt the Lord show me that these eunuchs were a prophetic picture of this generation. These are individuals who have battled oppression in their sexuality all their lives. When Jesus spoke about Jezebel, he specifically said that she seduces his servants to commit sexual immorality (Revelation 2:20). Combining Jesus' statement with our study in previous chapters on Jezebel's operation in the days of Elijah, I am convinced the spirit of Jezebel is the spirit behind all forms of sexual struggle.

The eunuchs had access to Jezebel in ways that no one else did; they knew her secrets and they knew her wickedness. She had deeply hurt them in a way and in a place that no one else had, and this hurt would undoubtedly have led to a feeling of shame, too. By castrating her eunuchs, Jezebel made their wound define their whole identity, which on one hand is a picture of purity but on the other hand is a picture of depravity. Let's take a look at both of these prophetic pictures, represented by the eunuchs under the oppression of Jezebel.

DEPRAVITY

Theologically, we can understand 'depravity' as the innate corruption of the human nature due to original sin. The eunuchs give us a picture of depravity in that they are symbols of one of Jezebel's main modes of operation – oppression, dysfunction and confusion in identity. The identity of the eunuch was tied to something that happened in their sexuality.

It's certainly not true of everyone, but a great percentage of the individuals I have met over the years who have struggled with some form of sexual battle – from pornography to sex addictions – have experienced some kind of trauma (mostly when they were younger) in the form of sexual abuse or exposure to images that planted a seed and began to pervert sex from God's original design and intention. Sometimes they recognised this as the starting point of their struggles, other times they didn't. Jezebel's entry point into our lives is often through a painful circumstance. For the eunuch, the wound is deep and shameful. The wounding was her pathway to binding the eunuchs to her and making them her slaves.

The eunuchs remind me of some people I know well, and many others I have met over the years. You may be reading this and feel like you can identify with the eunuchs. Perhaps your sexual identity has been wounded and you find yourself struggling with sexual addiction. Whatever has happened I want you to know there is hope for you to live in complete freedom. The manner in which the Lord used the eunuchs to destroy Jezebel gives me so much hope! I have seen the Lord deliver many people from the hold of sexual immorality or addiction. I too am a living testimony of his delivering power. Do not accept the status quo of compromise and an ongoing cycle of addiction. The enemy desires for you to miss God's purposes for your life. He can often perceive the call of God on the life of an individual and so he does his best to bind them before they get to bind him.

When Jesus was born, the enemy – through Herod – tried to kill him almost immediately by ordering the killing of all children aged two years and under:

> Then Herod, when he saw that he had been tricked by the wise men, became furious, and he sent and killed all the male children in Bethlehem and in all that region who were two years old or under, according to the time that he had ascertained from the wise men.
>
> — Matthew 2:16

I don't think it's a stretch to say that Herod's actions were inspired by the devil. The enemy knew of the prophecy the Lord spoke in the book of Genesis, when he was cursing the serpent for deceiving Eve:

> And I will put enmity between you and the woman,
> and between your offspring and hers;
> he will crush your head, and you will strike his heel.
>
> — Genesis 3:15 (NIV)

In this context, the offspring of the woman is a reference to Jesus Christ, specifically. He was destined to crush the head of the serpent. The devil knew this so he was trying all he could to stop it. The magnitude of Herod's massacre reflected the level of fear in the heart of the devil about the destiny of this child. Hundreds, maybe thousands of babies were killed.

In this way, satanic opposition is often an indication of prophetic potential. The devil does not go to fight where there are no spoils. Just as the enemy killed children *en masse* in the days of Jesus, in the same way he is releasing mass temptation, deviation and addiction today, over a generation. I believe this is a reaction of the enemy to the revelation that children and the youth have the potential to play a significant role in the move of God in these last days.

In several nations around the world, governments are beginning to pass laws that allow children to be instilled with sexual ideologies that are not aligned with God's design and intention, through the education system. Why such an aggressive attack of the enemy on the sexual identity of children? I believe it is because of the prophetic potential they carry. They are destined to throw Jezebel down. The enemy is scared of this and so he is attacking them first in an attempt to frustrate the plans and purposes of God. However, we are not ignorant of his devices (2 Corinthians 2:11). Even though the eunuchs were slaves to Jezebel, their destiny was to destroy her. They were just waiting for a Jehu to empower them by opening their eyes to the fact that their proximity to Jezebel was a strategic positioning, so that they would be able to inflict maximum damage on the kingdom of darkness. Could it be that the struggle many people experience with sexual sin is a pre-emptive strike of the enemy on their lives because of the Lord's calling on them to destroy the hold of Jezebel over a generation? As I look through scripture, reflect on my personal experience and recall testimonies from people I have met, I have come to believe this is the case.

As I said, the enemy does not go to fight where there are no spoils. I love hearing testimonies of how encounters with God have radically changed people's lives and caused them to move from a place of oppression and addiction to a place of freedom, where they are even being used by God to impact the lives of others in the very areas that they themselves struggled with.

I was recently invited to speak at a prophetic conference and, just before I got up, a young man was sharing his testimony of how an encounter with God had changed his life and how he had recently started a ministry in reaching out to the youth with the message of the gospel. Three years earlier, he had attempted suicide. A year later, he came out as gay and left his family home to pursue a lifestyle that stood in stark contrast to that of his parents, who were both pastors. He shared about how his struggle with this kind of lifestyle had led him to the brink of suicide but God had completely changed him. To my shock, at the end of his testimony he mentioned that this breakthrough happened at a Prayer Storm event, even though the leaders at the meeting and I knew nothing about it happening at the time. My mouth fell open and I was completely blown away. I later got the opportunity to speak with his parents, who confirmed the transformation that had taken place in his life.

Two years earlier, I had been invited to host a Prayer Storm meeting at his parents' church. At the end of the last session, I gave an altar call and invited people to surrender their lives to Jesus. I also led the congregation in some prayers to destroy the hold of the enemy over people's lives – whatever form that might take for the people gathered there. This young man was in that meeting, sitting at the back of the auditorium, wishing he was somewhere else. In his words:

> I was not in a good place. My head and my heart believed in God but I was angry that he 'made me this way.' I don't know how or when, but at some point I found myself on my knees at the altar. I remember thinking, 'What are you doing? You don't do this anymore.' At that moment, Jesus came and knelt next to me and put his arm around me and said, 'This is not who I made you to be' and then it was as if I saw every true prophetic word spoken over me becoming a reality. I cried, and I felt a pain in the pit of my stomach, but it was a good pain. I repented for my heart, my bitterness and hate towards God and my family. I knew then that I had been deceived and had come to believe a lie. After about 30 minutes, I went to my mum and told her what had happened, and she gathered my dad and some intercessors, and they took me upstairs and just prayed over me. Once again, I was repenting and crying. After a short time, I opened my eyes and everyone could immediately see that I

looked different. It was like the scales had fallen off and I could see clearly. Since then, I have never struggled with depression, with my identity or sexuality. I know who I am and whose I am.

To be honest, I am just as amazed as anyone else when I hear testimonies like this. In our prayer meetings, we always call people to surrender their lives fully to Jesus. There is always a call to consecration and living on fire for God, but in the process of people responding to the Lord, the Holy Spirit brings transformation to their lives in ways that completely blow our minds.

At another Prayer Storm gathering in Manchester a few years ago, we had an altar call for people who had suffered sexual abuse. There was a particular girl who came forward, and my wife, Rebecca, prayed for healing from sexual abuse and deliverance from rejection. This girl later came to Rebecca and seemed completely transformed. Rebecca had prayed, specifically, for healing from sexual abuse and deliverance from rejection, but the unfolding of this was that the girl seemed to have been released from something that had had a hold over her entire life, relationships and sense of identity. She declared that she no longer found men sickening, which was quite surprising given the extreme physical aversion she had been feeling, and that she wasn't experiencing same-sex attraction anymore. After some time, she decided to grow her hair from the short cut she'd always had, and didn't feel uncomfortable dressing in a more feminine way. Of course, clothes are just clothes and hair is just hair, but what was clear was that she now felt at peace with her own identity and was no longer oppressed by that internal conflict. No longer was her whole self-identity defined by the sexual abuse that had been inflicted upon her.

Let me recognise, at this point, that you may well be struggling in this area right now, or you may know someone who's really having a hard time, and what you read in this chapter may make you feel very discouraged or upset. I want you to know that my intention in sharing this is to give you abounding hope. I also have friends who are working this out and have prayed and sought the Lord, and have still not seen any dramatic changes like the testimonies I have shared here. Sometimes deliverance is a dramatic, instantaneous break-through, and other times it is a process. Either way, we fix our eyes on Jesus: the author and finisher of our faith. I love this scripture from Hebrews 4:15-16: 'For we do not have a High Priest who cannot sympathise with our weaknesses, but was in all points tempted as we are, yet without sin. Let us there-fore come boldly to the throne of grace, that we may obtain mercy and find grace to help in time of need.' If you need prayer and support, be sure to speak to someone you trust. In the next chapter, I discuss in more detail the importance of accountability and community in breaking the hold of the enemy over our lives, whatever form that takes for us.

Jesus was full of grace and truth. He wasn't just full of truth or just full of grace; it was a combination of both grace and truth. The conversations that go on amongst some Christians about the LGBTQ community are so often lacking in either one of these areas, but one without the other is damaging and dangerous. Grace without truth leads to moral decline, causing people to be blind to their need for repentance and for Jesus. Truth without grace ends up crushing people, which leads to a legalistic self-righteousness. Like Jesus, we have to be full of both grace and truth.

There is a huge amount of division among Christians about what the biblical response should be towards this community. Some respond in what looks like hatred, lack of empathy and love, claiming that anyone identifying with this community is of the devil and going to hell, while others respond in what looks like tolerance and seem to accept the LGBTQ lifestyle. They reason that social norms and culture have changed over the years and we, as Christians, should keep up and accept this or else we are not loving but judging others.

Christians are often portrayed as homophobic, hating anyone who identifies as homosexual. In many cases, this perception is absolutely justified because so many from the Church have expressed hatred and vitriol towards this community. This is painfully sad, and does not reflect the heart of God. On the other hand, the LGBTQ community – and sections of the secular media – tends to react very strongly and passionately against anyone who does not agree with their lifestyle. So, for fear of being labelled anti-gay or homophobic, many Christians keep silent and refuse to engage with this community.

I think it is possible for us to be honest about our stance on what the scriptures teach about sexuality, while also walking in love and compassion towards individuals who are facing challenge in these areas. We should not lower the standard of scripture in conformity to culture. We are called to be ambassadors for Christ to culture and a people full of grace and truth. We need to get this settled in our hearts, once and for all: the word of God will never be politically correct. As long as our desire is to become popular, in the cultural sense, we will continue to lower the standard of scripture, watering it down so as to fit in.

The issues surrounding many individuals who identify as LGBTQ are extremely complex, and it is not my intention here to delve deeply into this topic or to make sweeping statements; it is more to speak hope and prophecy into what I believe the Lord is going to do amongst this community. I believe that many in the LGBTQ community don't realise that there is such a strong call of God on their lives. The enemy wants them to feel rejected by God and those he has anointed, like Jehu, to bring about their freedom.

I believe those identifying as lesbian, gay, bisexual, transgender and queer are going to experience a powerful move of God in these days. Just as the eunuchs played a vital role in destroying the influence of Jezebel over a generation, I believe these individuals will play a similarly critical role in striking a blow that inflicts maximum damage to the kingdom of darkness. There is a move of the Holy Spirit brewing over the LGBTQ community. The Jehus need to arise from the secret place, anointed by the Holy Spirit, to empower them to throw Jezebel down.

Later, we will confront what I believe is the most significant weapon Jezebel has unleashed over our generation, and that is pornography. However, to conclude this chapter I'd like to explore the other prophetic picture that I believe the eunuchs represent, and that is sexual purity.

PURITY STANDARDS

The eunuchs were unable to partake in any form of sexual immorality because their sexual organs had been removed. I see this as a picture of sexual purity. I also think this can be representative of purity in other areas: purity of heart, motives and intentions, for example. Purity is one of the most significant weapons we have in our arsenal against Jezebel.

Jesus gives us an insight into his standard for purity in Matthew 5. This teaching really did shift the goal posts and would have been striking to his audience at the time, but it is just as challenging to put into practice today:

> You have heard that it was said to those of old, 'You shall not commit adultery.' But I say to you that whoever looks at a woman to lust for her has already committed adultery with her in his heart. If your right eye causes you to sin, pluck it out and cast it from you; for it is more profitable for you that one of your

members perish, than for your whole body to be cast
into hell. And if your right hand causes you to sin, cut
it off and cast it from you; for it is more profitable for
you that one of your members perish, than for your
whole body to be cast into hell.

— Matthew 5:27–30

Jesus was not by any means promoting self-mutilation. In
context, we can see that as far as he was concerned adultery
was not just a physical act; it was a sin that happened first
in the heart. So, in essence, our imaginations are his reality.
The eye looks at pornography not because it has a will of its
own but because the heart is full of lust. The deeper issue here
is the heart behind the action. Jesus was using hyperbole to
stress the seriousness of sin and the need to make exceptional
sacrifices if we want to live pure. That's why some people
take such seemingly extreme steps as getting rid of computers,
phones, TVs and the internet in order to cut off the enemy's
access in their lives, through areas of weakness that they have
identified in their soul.

The essence of what Jesus was saying in Matthew 5 is
challenging us to have a radical approach to pursuing purity
of the heart, giving the enemy no access points. The eunuchs
having their sexual organs removed mirrors this passage
because it communicates to us the importance of cutting away
everything that the enemy may have access to in our lives in
order to pursue purity. Those who threw Jezebel down were

completely disconnected from her main tool of seduction –
sexual immorality.

> ...the ruler of this world is coming, and he has nothing
> in me.
>
> — John 14:30

Jesus was able to defeat the enemy because the enemy had
nothing in Jesus that was of his kingdom. Holiness is a
weapon of warfare against the kingdom of darkness. Spiritual
warfare is not always as obvious and in your face as we might
imagine. When we live in holiness, our very presence becomes
a rebuke to darkness because the light we carry in our spirit is
able to shine through our souls much more easily. We cannot
entertain any of the traits of Jezebel in our lives and at the
same time try to throw her down. As I said earlier, it is impossible to have authority over an enemy that you're sleeping
with.

If you have found this chapter hard to read, or you are
struggling with any of the things I have touched upon here,
I really want to encourage you: I believe your struggle is a
pre-emptive strike of the enemy on your life because of your
calling to destroy the hold of Jezebel. You don't have to settle
for Jezebel's seduction and ongoing cycles of temptation and
addiction. There is freedom in the name of Jesus. In the next
chapter I'll be sharing my own testimony and some guiding
principles for walking in the purity and authority necessary
to throw Jezebel down.

CONTENDING IN PRAYER, PURITY AND POWER

I t felt like I had let the Lord down once again, and the feeling of shame and disappointment with myself was so overwhelming. All I could think was, how did I end up here again? I had promised the Lord I'd never do this again and now here I was, like a dog returning to its vomit. Oh God help me!

I did ask for God's mercy and tried to repent in the best way I knew how, but this felt like a recurring behaviour and I was beginning to believe the lie that God was tired of forgiving me. This lie of the enemy was easier for me to believe because, even while I was praying, I could still sense the hold of lust on my mind. There was this strange but familiar sense that I would be back in a few weeks' time, going through the same ritual of asking God for help.

I don't remember exactly how old I was when I was first exposed to pornography, but I'm convinced it was before I turned 13. At the time I didn't know what pornography was, but I'd found some pictures in the neighbourhood, somewhere close to my parents' house, and found them fascinating. I obviously didn't understand what was going on with my body but it just felt to me like something I wanted to do more of, and in secret.

Many people who are addicted to pornography would say that it was pretty much immediate, after their very first exposure. My experience was quite different. I didn't seem to have any connection or addiction to pornography until my late teens, and that's when it became a recurring problem in my life.

When I discovered just how easily I could access pornography online it became so much easier to feed this addiction in secret. I was actively involved in serving at my local church but this was a part of my life I certainly didn't want anyone knowing anything about. I wasn't looking at pornography every day, but the recurring nature of my visits to pornographic sites (at this time, probably once or twice a month) made me realise I was addicted. I tried all kinds of things to break out of this addiction, including downloading software that would block access to certain sites. There were times that I would go for two, three, sometimes six months without visiting a pornographic website, but then I would hit a moment of weakness and it was as though I was paralysed in my will and ability to resist. I was a slave to lust.

This went on for several years and then one day I felt like God showed me a way out. I felt that I had to expose this recurring sin to my dad. How embarrassing! I plucked up the courage to speak with him about my struggle, and I thought he'd be really mad at me. Thankfully, he wasn't, and instead he spoke some words of wisdom and prayed over me. I can't say that I felt a sudden bolt of lightning or anything spectacular like that at the time, but I noticed that several years went by without me experiencing that familiar paralysis of my will when a moment of weakness collided with temptation from the enemy. Now, at the time of writing, it's been over 10 years since I last visited a pornographic site. This is a testament to the delivering power of God. What really blew my mind was that, after being delivered, I struggled to remember any of the images I'd seen. I believe the blood of Jesus cleansed my mind from all pornographic and Jezebelic contaminations and influences. Praise God!

My dad gave me one of the best pieces of advice I had ever heard on dealing with temptation. He said to me, 'James, don't just come and confess to me when you have fallen into sin and looked at porn. I want you to call me or text me the very moment you feel the temptation so strongly that you know that your next move would probably lead to a pornographic site. In that moment, get in touch with me and ask for prayer.' Wow! He was asking me to not just focus on confessing after I had sinned but to practise confessing and exposing the temptation before falling into it. Following his advice made me realise that bringing the sin out into the light, exposing it in this way, dramatically reduced its power and paralysing effect.

The real power of sin often lies in its secrecy. Learning to expose sin is one of the ways we can break agreement with the enemy. He is known as the prince of darkness. He loves to work in the dark. We are children of the light so we really cannot and should not have fellowship with darkness. We have to expose darkness. It is in our DNA to expose and eradicate darkness. In Ephesians 5:11, Paul tells us to 'have no fellowship with the unfruitful works of darkness, but rather expose them.'

I believe the spirit behind all forms of pornography is Jezebel: a spirit of lust and seduction. With pornography being so readily accessible these days, millions of people have come under the seduction and bondage of Jezebel. If you are struggling with pornography, or other forms of sexual addiction, I'd like to encourage you to pray and ask the Lord about who he has placed in your life at this time to walk alongside you in the light. Be aware that this is a decision that shouldn't be taken lightly – confessing to the wrong people can be disastrous! Nonetheless, we must make a personal commitment to walk in the light and have no fellowship with darkness, and we must practise accountability.

THE POWER OF TOGETHERNESS

Walking in the light, we don't walk alone. We are not living in isolation from community. In fact, in contending for purity, we must make it a priority to journey alongside others. I find it interesting that it wasn't just one lone eunuch who made the decision to throw Jezebel down; two or three eunuchs listened to Jehu.

> And he looked up at the window, and said, 'Who is on my side? Who?' So two or three eunuchs looked out at him.
>
> — 2 Kings 9:32

It has always intrigued me that every translation of this verse says 'two or three'. How come the writer of Kings couldn't specify an exact number? After all, it's not that difficult to differentiate between two and three people. It was either two or three eunuchs that threw her down. I am convinced this verse was written in this way because it emphasises one of the strategies for throwing Jezebel down – two or three. Many years after the death of Queen Jezebel, Jesus taught his disciples about the power of two or three:

> For where two or three are gathered together in my name, I am there in the midst of them.
>
> — Matthew 18:20

This verse shows us what is available when we meet together in his name. It invokes a manifestation of his presence. This speaks of what we often call 'the corporate anointing', but it also highlights accountability. The magnitude of Jezebel's influence meant that bringing her down wasn't going to be a one man job. It had to be two or three coming together in agreement. Again, this not only emphasises the need to walk in the light but it shows us that we have to throw her down together.

The Church is meant to be a place where people who are struggling with sin and addiction can come to find freedom. But, more often, it seems to be the place where everyone pretends they're okay and they have no issues. So people end up putting virtual masks on at church and not being real with one another. It's so sad that people with broken hearts and lives often don't feel that church is a place where they can be real. Imagine if hospitals had such a reputation that sick people didn't want to go because they thought the doctors would make them feel ashamed.

This is a crucial hour for the Church to be real with itself and acknowledge that there is a great deal of brokenness and addiction in our midst. Jezebel may not be a physical person, whispering in the ear of the church leader and trying to dominate and control the congregation (although this is certainly one manifestation), but many churches have already forfeited their authority and been neutralised by Jezebel because of their tolerance for secret sexual sins. We will not be able to destroy her influence over the Church without the reality of purity, accountability and unity. Throwing Jezebel down will take more than one person – it will take two or three.

We are not called the body of Jesus, but rather the body of Christ. The word Christ means 'the anointed one'. Jesus is the head, and we are the body. I believe there is a fullness of the manifestation of Christ (the anointing) that is only seen when there is a coming together of the body. In other words, there are dimensions of breakthrough that we will not see until the body begins to function as one.

WATCH AND PRAY

Jesus says to us in Mark 14:38, 'Watch and pray, lest you enter into temptation.' To watch, here, means to be alert, vigilant, awake. We do this in the spirit.

In other words, we are meant to be discerning the activities going on around us in the realm of the spirit, as well as being aware of the condition of our souls while we pray. Just as the watchmen had the responsibility of sounding the alarm to warn of impending danger, when we pray we are meant to watch in the spirit and then respond accordingly.

Notice that Jesus didn't say, 'Watch and pray, lest you *avoid* temptation.' He said, 'Watch and pray, lest you *enter into* temptation.' The prayers that enable us to overcome temptations are not so much the prayers that are uttered in the depths of the struggle, but the prayers that we pray before the temptation arises. In choosing to have zero tolerance for the spirit of Jezebel in our lives, we need to develop a strong prayer life.

Developing a strong prayer life is like going to the gym. The consistent application of the basics leads to dramatic gains over time. Make time for prayer every day. Start with what you can manage, and as you grow in the quality of your time with the Lord you will also want to grow in quantity. It is impossible to stay pure and overcome this spirit of seduction without a prayer life. In fact, the weaker and less consistent you are in prayer the more susceptible you are to Jezebel's attacks. It's one thing to get free and quite another to stay free. Prayer energises your spirit; it equips and empowers your spirit to rule your soul, thereby making it easier to resist temptations when they arise.

As believers, we have spiritual weapons for warfare. In the book of Corinthians, Paul sheds some light on what our weapons actually do in the spirit realm when deployed against the kingdom of darkness.

> For the weapons of our warfare are not carnal but mighty in God for pulling down *strongholds*, casting down *arguments* and every *high thing* that *exalts* itself against the knowledge of God, bringing every thought into captivity to the obedience of Christ, and being ready to punish all disobedience when your obedience is fulfilled.
>
> — 2 Corinthians 10:4 (emphasis added)

When Jehu entered the gate, Jezebel started talking to him, but he refused to engage in any conversation with her. He first looked up because Jezebel was in an exalted position, and he was probably considering his strategy for getting to her. In the natural order of things, her position gave her an advantage over Jehu – she was looking down on him – but Jehu was about to literally enact 2 Corinthians 10:4. Jezebel was a 'stronghold' in the nation, she was releasing 'arguments' to him and she was in a 'high' place because she had exalted herself against the knowledge of God among the people. This was the end for Jezebel. Jehu's weapons of warfare were not carnal; they were made mighty in God because he was anointed in the secret place. He was commissioned by the Lord to pull down the stronghold of Jezebel, cast down her arguments, and take her projections captive (high security at the gate!).

It is unavoidable that if we are going to destroy the stranglehold of Jezebel over our lives, families, communities and nation we will need to engage in spiritual warfare, and we must ready ourselves for that.

STAND OUT, RISE UP AND THROW HER DOWN

I started this book by sharing about my 11:11 encounter with the Lord. That encounter awakened me to what I believe is one of the most critical battles the people of God will face on the earth in the end times, before the return of Jesus. Carrying the spirit of Elijah, John the Baptist was used by God to prepare the way for the first coming of Jesus. In the same way, the spirit of Elijah will rest upon a generation to prepare the way for the second coming of Jesus.

I believe that generation will look like John in their radical pursuit and devotion to the Lord. Elijah didn't complete his assignment, and John the Baptist was beheaded. Both Elijah and John were up against a wicked spirit of seduction: Jezebel.

In these last days the Lord is raising up a new breed of believers who will overthrow the altars of Baal and have zero tolerance for Jezebel's seductions, who will possess the gates of the enemy and destroy the stranglehold of Jezebel over a generation, and who will usher in the greatest move of the Holy Spirit the world has ever seen.

In these last days God is raising up a new breed of believers that will carry the spirit of Elijah just like John the Baptist did to prepare the way for the second coming of Jesus.

Is your heart stirred to be a part of this army of the Lord? Then it's time to be fully awake and consecrated to him. It's time to enter the fight we were born for by cultivating intimacy with God in the secret place of prayer and purity of heart as we increase the security system at our gates. The Lord is calling you to live a life on fire!

When God has a special mission he often places a demand on a life for a special lifestyle. This new breed of warriors being raised up are called to a special lifestyle of consecration. When we capture a true revelation of his eyes of fire, we are empowered to overcome the spirit of seduction in our culture and will be entrusted with authority over nations (Revelation 2:26). His eyes of fire empower us to live a life on fire.

What is coming is nothing short of a fight for the soul of the nation. If you are going to be one of the 'two or three' who will throw Jezebel down and release a freedom and a peace that passes from generation to generation, you are going to have to stand out and rise up. If this sounds scary or over-whelming, that's okay. Now is the time to prepare yourself in the secret place and to shore up the security at your gates. Perhaps you have already had your 11:11 moment, or perhaps it's still to come.

Watch and pray, and be ready.

PRAYER STORM

Storm is a movement of worship,
yer and fasting which exists to
voke a spiritual awakening by
ng an army of praying warriors.

Join the movement:

PRAYERSTORM.ORG

PRAYER
STORM

EXPERIENCE THE BATTLE CRY

Featuring 10 tracks with worship led by Rebecca Aladiran, Lisa Burrell and spoken word prayers by James Aladiran.

shop.prayerstorm.org

NOTES

NOTES

NOTES

NOTES

NOTES

NOTES

NOTES

NOTES